RUNDI

Hand rearing baby elephants

Catherine Buckle

Published by Catherine Buckle
P.O. Box 842
Marondera, Zimbabwe
Email: cbuckle.zim@gmail.com
www.cathybuckle.com
©Catherine Buckle, 2016
ISBN : 978-0-7974-7102-3

Also by Catherine Buckle:
African Tears
Beyond Tears
Innocent Victims
Imire, the life and times of Norman Travers
Can you Hear the Drums? Letters from Zimbabwe 2000–2004
Millions, Billions, Trillions. Letters from Zimbabwe 2005–2009
Sleeping Like a Hare

Cover design: Graham van de Ruit (www.grahamvdr.com)
Design and typesetting: Graham van de Ruit
Front and back cover photographs: Ian Buckle
Text photographs: Ian Buckle
Fierynecked nightjar illustration: © Margaret Shattock

In memory of Oscar, Raymond, Simon and Joçam

ACKNOWLEDGEMENTS

Thank you:

Ian Buckle for photographs and memories.

Carolyn Dennison for contributions, answering questions and help in unearthing archives long forgotten.

Pete Taylor, Margaret Matejcic and Terry Fallon for memories, anecdotes and encouragement.

Roaland Jooste, Morna Knottenbelt and Sally Claasen in absentia for help, advice and friendship.

Rolf Chenaux Repond for helpful advice with technical matters regarding the deepening of the pan.

Andre Groenewald for time, advice and layman's explanation of falcons and falconry.

Simon Pitt, Chairman of the Mukuvisi Wodlands for his enthusiasm and encouragement.

ONE

....

When the side-door of the truck finally swung open, the view in the torchlight was of three large grey backsides. It had taken almost half an hour for the noisy, smoky vehicle to be manoeuvred into position and the three occupants in the back weren't happy at all. The door of the truck had to be absolutely flush with the unloading ramp; that's what had taken so long because even the smallest gap which could allow a foot to get wedged would be disastrous. A fog of dust and diesel smoke hung in the night air making the first view of elephant backsides arriving in the capital city very surreal. This wasn't a zoo, it was the place we called 'A touch of the wild in the heart of the city,' and this precious cargo arriving in the dead of night, was about to change everyone's lives.

There were six of us waiting in the dark for the baby elephants, ready to guide them out of the truck, down the ramp and into the secure enclosure that was to be their temporary home. There was nothing normal about what was going on. These elephants weren't tame, had never seen a city, a truck or even a human being until a couple of days ago. They were newly orphaned wild babies, survivors of elephant culling operations in the lowveld of Zimbabwe. For more than half an hour we tried to persuade the elephants to leave the truck but they weren't budging. Their grey backsides filled the doorway sending us a visual message which spoke volumes. Calling, cajoling, whistling and even complete silence didn't work and so we laid a trail of ground-nut hay and horse cubes from the door of the crate, down the ramp and all the way into the boma.

Everyone kept very quiet and still until at last, fifteen long minutes later, the sweet smell of food tempted the elephants to investigate. A little trunk dropped down and sniffed between grey legs, then another long nose and another until the first tentative steps were taken.

Slowly, nervously, the elephants turned around and walked off the truck, following the line of food. As soon as they went past me and out of sight down the dark, high, grass-walled passage towards the enclosure, we pushed poles across the gateway at the top of the ramp, closing off the exit and the truck. Thuds, thumps, curses and grunts could be heard from the darkness as three men guided the elephants to the secure circular stockade where food, water and giant hay-beds awaited. There was no turning back for the elephants now, or for me. For at least the next two years I was committed and would eat, sleep and think baby elephants twenty four hours a day.

The three baby elephants that arrived at the Mukuvisi Woodlands game park in August 1986 were injured, visibly traumatized and very frightened. Standing only as high as my waist, they were covered in oozing wounds, plastered in dung and completely unapproachable. They were estimated to be just five months old and had a fine fuzz of soft black hair on the top of their heads and down their backs. Their trunks were floppy, particularly that of the little female who didn't seem to have much control of her nose at all!

The time span between their capture in the lowveld and arrival at the Harare game park was forty eight hours. In that time they had been restrained with ropes, pushed, shoved and manhandled into crates and trucks and then driven hundreds of kilometres across bumpy, dusty roads. For the duration of the journey the elephants had only been given water occasionally but no food; it was a very long time for un-weaned animals to go without milk from their mothers. In the wild, elephant calves suckle for up to two years and because these five month old baby elephants were being weaned at such a dangerously early age, their survival was far from being guaranteed.

Once the three elephant calves were safely secured in the small circular stockade at the centre of the boma we left them alone; they needed time to calm down and recover from the enormous stress and trauma of the past two days. Our security guards patrolled around the boma day and night to make sure no one, man or beast, got in or out and the next morning our work began.

Because the elephants were so wild and scared they weren't allowed out of their stockade at first and so everything was done through narrow gaps between the poles in their small circular holding pen. Although the elephant calves had mostly depended on their mothers' milk to survive until now, in the wild they began eating vegetation from about three or four months of age and so we started with something simple. Half a sack of cabbage leaves were pushed through the gap in the poles and it didn't take long for the elephants to realise that even though this food was unfamiliar, it smelled sweet and tasted good. The elephants were extremely suspicious of people and wouldn't come anywhere near the food until they couldn't see or smell humans. Simon and I retreated, climbing the narrow wooden steps that led to a small observation deck high above the stockade. From there we could see everything very clearly but not be seen.

Simon was the 'elephant man' of the Mukuvisi Woodlands. He had reared 'Coke' the now huge female elephant who had come to the Woodlands three years before as a baby, another terrified survivor of culling operations. Simon did everything for the elephants: feeding, cleaning, walking and caring for them. He had a gentle but firm hand, always caring and compassionate, never cruel, violent or vindictive.

In his late thirties Simon was a quiet, soft spoken man who took his time to get things done but when it came to the elephants nothing was too much for him. Simon's passions included a few drinks over the weekends, in fact often more than a few drinks, and his home-made cigarettes which were filled with dubious tobacco sweepings and other mysterious things, loosely rolled in scraps of newspaper. Side by side we stood on the lofty platform above the boma, looking down on the three new baby elephants and watched in silence.

The biggest of the three elephant calves came towards the pile of cabbage leaves. He shook his head, ears slapping noisily against his neck and sniffed the air in all directions with his trunk half raised. A few more quick glances around and a couple of deep sniffs and then hunger replaced suspicion. Leaf after leaf was picked up with the tip of his trunk and pushed into the elephant's mouth. Perhaps it was the sight of one elephant eating, or the crunching sound of leaves being chewed but it wasn't long before the second calf, also a male, approached the cabbage pile and began to eat. The last baby elephant, much smaller than the other two, and a female, was far more hesitant. She spent a long time watching, sniffing and looking around, obviously suspicious and nervous. She took two steps forward and then reversed. Twice more she stepped forwards and reversed until, when there was almost no food left, the little female got close enough to pick up one small, trampled cabbage leaf. She definitely wasn't as adept as the others when it came to the use of her trunk and at the first attempt in getting cabbage leaf from nose to mouth, the little elephant missed altogether and the leaf fell to the ground. Her second attempt was equally unsuccessful and as her trunk sought out the fallen leaf, it was snatched up by one of the other elephants and then there was nothing left for her to find. Her frustration and hunger exploded and the little female bellowed and swung her backside into one of the other elephants. We could hear the thump from our hiding place and watched horrified as all three elephants started pushing and shoving each other, bumping and trumpeting. There was nothing we could do except watch from our elevated vantage point and be thankful that their stockade was circular and made of poles. There were no corners to get stuck in, nothing protruding to cause injuries and nothing sharp or angular on which the elephants could hurt themselves. Even their water container was soft: a huge rubber tractor tyre that had been reshaped, opened out and made into a perfect, soft, elephant proof drinking trough.

Feeding the baby elephants was a delicate, complex matter; too much of a new food could cause diarrhoea or colic and too little would lead to starvation and malnutrition. We immediately began to introduce them to a new diet of largely unfamiliar foods. They had come from the hot, dry, scratchy lowveld where the landscape was dominated by the strange, upside down Baobab trees (*Adansonia digitata*), Mopane trees (*Colophospermum mopane*) with their distinctive butterfly wing shaped leaves and Sausage trees (*Kigelia Africana*) whose giant pendulous fruits hang down in spectacular display, defying you to rest underneath and risk being hit a by a 10 kg sausage fruit. Now the elephants were in the much cooler, greener Highveld in Miombo woodland where there were marshes, wetlands and vleis alongside drier woodland where Musasa (*Brachystigia spiciformis*) and Munondo (*Julbernardia globiflora*) trees dominated. It was here that the baby elephants would later discover the delights of wild oranges, mahobohobos and mbola plums. At the moment everything was strange and unknown to these elephants, from the temperature and altitude to the sounds, smells and most of the vegetation. The secret with the food was going to be to only give the elephants a little at time, making sure they didn't get diarrhoea; we had to give their digestive systems time to get used to the new diet.

We fed them every three hours on that first day: the outer dark green, sweet cabbage leaves; young leaves and stems of wild reeds which grew in marshy wetland and a variety of leaves from indigenous trees in the Woodlands. Everything had to be found, picked, cut, collected and carried back to the boma for the elephants in 50 kg sacks. It was a full time job for two workers who were under strict instruction from Simon who knew exactly what he wanted for 'his babies,' along with how much he wanted and when.

"Right Simon, let's go over this list," I said, anxious to get started in gathering the ingredients that formed the less natural but equally critical part of the elephants diet.

"Four loaves of bread

Two kilos of milk powder

A dozen oranges

Two sacks of cabbage leaves

Two kilos of porridge."

Simon nodded in agreement and I set off to do the shopping: cabbage leaves and oranges from Honeydew Farm; porridge, milk powder and bread from a supermarket. I had to smile as I wondered what the tellers in the supermarket would think if they could see the heading on my shopping list: 'Elephants: breakfast, lunch, supper: one day.'

The work began as soon as I returned with all the items on my list. Simon carefully checked everything I'd bought. We laid it out on empty sacks in a shady corner of the boma and he muttered and nodded as he inspected everything, satisfied with what I'd got. He looked up and smiled his approval, I had passed the test. By now Simon had got the message that I wasn't going anywhere, didn't mind long hours or getting wet, smelly or dirty and that we were in this together. Cutting a couple of oranges in half, we blotted the wet, dripping surfaces into the milk powder. The sweet, cream-coloured milk powder stuck to the damp surface of the orange halves. Both ingredients were as important as each other: the oranges were full of natural vitamin C; the milk powder was going to be the basis for the formula we would introduce to the elephants as a substitute for their mothers' milk.

Standing a couple of metres apart Simon and I chose places where we could get our forearms in between the poles of the boma stockade and we placed the milk-dipped orange segments carefully on the ground. If we had put all the food in one place, there was no way all three elephants would be able to get their share and fighting was bound to break out again. It didn't take long before the strong citrus smell attracted the three elephants who came slowly and suspiciously towards the food. Simon and I kept completely still where we were and although the elephants probably couldn't see us, they could definitely smell us and just wouldn't come and pick up the oranges.

Peeling another orange, I broke it into segments, threw some in, whispering to Simon to do the same:

"Try and throw them far into the enclosure Simon."

"But what about the milk powder? They must have the milk."

"Yes, I know, but let's get them eating first and when they've got a taste for the oranges, we'll try the pieces dipped in milk powder."

Simon looked at me with raised eyebrows: he had been through all this before with Coke and knew what he was doing. I could almost hear him thinking: 'who are you to tell me how to do my job?' But I didn't meet his eyes; all I could see were the great clusters of flies feeding on the oozing, pus-filled wounds that were all over the elephants, on their legs, feet, backs and heads. We just had to get these elephants eating and calmed down quickly so that their sores could be treated.

The elephants rapidly demolished the few segments of orange that we had thrown in and I threw some more pieces in, closer to us this time. Again they ate them although I noticed that the little female wasn't getting anything, she was just too slow and timid.

"OK Simon, try your milk powder now," I whispered. The elephants had a taste for the citrus and were still hungry.

Simon dipped more orange halves in milk powder, pushed them through the gap and it worked a treat, the two bigger animals snatching up all the fruit immediately. Still the little female hadn't eaten. Simon climbed up the cross poles of the stockade and threw half a sack of cabbage leaves into the enclosure to attract the two bigger elephants and lure them away. The plan worked and with the two males busy in the cabbage pile, Simon concentrated on the little female: dipping pieces of orange in milk powder and throwing them right at her feet. Again and again she charged at the poles, raising clouds of dust that settled like talcum powder all over Simon's hair, face and shoulders. The female elephant was suspicious of everything but at last she picked up a dusty orange segment and put it into her mouth. We held our breath. Simon threw another segment; again the elephant charged and reversed but then picked up the fruit and ate it. I noticed that she would often swing her trunk backwards and forwards and up and down and couldn't help but smile at her antics with her rubbery, wiggly trunk. Seeing her finally start eating I knew that the ice had been broken.

This feeding routine was repeated every two hours for the rest of the day. I was dispatched to get more oranges and we very soon understood that if she was going to survive, the female elephant had to be fed individually, away from the competition of the two males. We adjusted our methods accordingly and all day worked on the next ingredient on their menu: soggy bread.

With Simon on one side of the ring paddock and me on the other, each of us loaded with food, my job was to keep the two males out of the way. They weren't nearly as timid or temperamental as the female; they were just hungry so my job was to be a feeding machine, shoving food through to them between the poles. I couldn't touch either of the elephants and didn't want to try, in case it scared them and slowed down progress, so I just kept on dropping food through the poles in their direction.

Simon took on the challenge of the female; he had a lot more experience than me when it came to facing down temperamental baby elephants and dusty, stone-flicking mock charges. Simon put both his arms through gaps in the poles and called to the female. Sniffing the air, smelling the food but seeing only Simon's arms, the female elephant immediately started her charge. Instead of stopping and reversing when she reached the poles, the elephant skidded to a stop millimetres from where Simon stood on the other side of the poles.

Horrified I watched as the elephant lifted her trunk, reached forward and grabbed Simon's arm. Was this the same little elephant that I didn't think really knew what to do with her trunk, I wondered? I was sure I was about to see a broken arm about to happen but it was too late to intervene and I watched helplessly. I suppose it was just as well that I didn't know in advance that this was all part of Simon's plan; I'm sure I would have insisted this was far too dangerous. I didn't think the female elephant had much strength in her trunk but I was wrong! While the elephant held his arm with her trunk, Simon stretched forward and put his other hand, balled into a fist, right into her mouth. In his fist he held a wad of soggy bread that had been soaked in milk and thick porridge. Moments later he pulled his hand out, covered in slime and saliva but minus the bread.

"Ha! We are winning!" he said, a huge grin across his face.

My task was much easier, dropping chunks of soggy, milk-saturated bread through the poles which were snatched up by the two males almost as fast I could dispense them. Once we were both satisfied that the elephants had all had their share of milk-soaked food, piles of green reed tips, freshly picked leaves, horse cubes and hay were thrown in over the top of the poles and they were left alone.

One feeding session would sometimes take up to an hour and at the end of it we would both be filthy; Simon more so than me, and his arm was soon swollen and covered with bruises from the pulling and wrenching of the little female. The times the elephants were left alone had been significantly reduced. The quicker they got used to us, to new noises, smells and foods, the sooner we would be able to treat their wounds and prepare them for release into the game park.

On the third day, with another load of 'groceries' for the elephants at the ready, we worked on getting the calves to eat from our hands. This was all part of the process of getting the elephants used to having direct contact with people. We needed to be able to touch them, treat their wounds and tame them down, and they needed to get used to being handled. The two bigger elephants were not a problem: snatching soggy wads of bread out of Simon's hand faster than he could supply it. The little female was still suspicious and nervous so while Simon concentrated on her I again fed the other two through a gap in the poles on the other side of the stockade from where I had a good view of the back end of the female elephant and the numerous wounds on her rump, legs and feet.

At last, after much coaxing, the female came towards Simon, mock charged a couple of times and hastily snatched the bread from his flat, open palm and immediately reversed a few paces. We watched as she lifted her trunk to her mouth, sucked off the sticky mess of bread and porridge and put her trunk forward to get more. Simon and I looked at each other through the poles from opposite sides of the ring stockade and we both grinned at this huge step forward. Soggy, porridgy bread was high on the menu for the rest of the day; they had a taste for it now and we were thrilled. Milk buckets were next.

Finally the time had arrived for a face to face meeting with the elephants.

"I want to get in!" Simon announced when I arrived the next morning.

"Do you think they're ready?"

"I want to try," Simon said, giving me his wide, toothless grin. "If it's OK then you can come and help me in the afternoon," he announced.

Simon looked exhausted, his eyes bloodshot from lack of sleep.

These first few days of being responsible for keeping three wild elephants alive and calming them down was taking its toll on him. We definitely needed to get them started on drinking milk as soon as possible and Simon was determined he should be the first one to get into the circular enclosure with the elephants. This was a dangerous operation: one man in a small circular pen with three wild elephant calves; all sorts of things could go wrong from pushing and shoving to crushing, being knocked over and even trampled. I felt very nervous about what might happen, these three elephants may have been babies but they were also wild, unpredictable and frightened; they could very easily kill him. I insisted that the other workers be ready nearby in case a hasty rescue was needed.

"You can go in Simon but let's make sure everything's ready first. If you go and call all the others, I'll prepare the milk bucket."

We agreed that only one milk bucket would be made up because there was a very good chance it would end up on the ground and Simon needed to have one hand free to grab onto poles and scramble out of the way if necessary. In a strong galvanised bucket I mixed together measured quantities of Pronutro instant porridge flakes and milk powder, added a little water , stirred until all the lumps were gone and then added enough water to half fill the bucket to about eight litres.

The other workers arrived: Oscar, the foreman, my right hand man who had taught me so much but who was not awfully comfortable around elephants; Joçam , the hardest, fastest worker I'd ever encountered and a man who was totally fearless; Raymond, a very gentle, gentleman, always willing to help but often intimidated by the sheer size and power of animals, and Leonard, our security guard, an enormously tall man, a giant in all regards and someone who was always at the front in times of trouble. Together we were the team, the new family for the elephants, their new herd. There would be many other people involved in their lives in the next two years but for now we were the ones in close daily contact, the people that these elephants needed to bond with.

When everyone was ready and knew what to do if the worst happened, Simon prepared to open the gate. The gate was made of poles which lay horizontally across a portion of the enclosure; they were slotted into brackets and could be slid backwards and forwards to make an opening. Simon slid two poles out at the bottom, crouched down and squeezed into the circular stockade. Everyone kept quiet and still so as not to scare the elephants and I bent down and passed the bucket of milk through the opening. Three trunks came up and sniffed Simon and he stood quite still. When nothing happened, Simon started talking softly to the elephants; they were used to his smell and his voice by now and he held the bucket out towards them. After what seemed like ages but was actually only a minute or two, the tip of a trunk stretched forward and touched the bucket. Very slowly Simon tipped the bucket a little so that the milky porridge was closer to the trunk. The little grey nose dipped into the milk. One small, noisy slurp, a curled lifted trunk and the elephant poured the milk into its mouth. The noise was heaven to our ears and even though I couldn't see Simon's face I knew he would be grinning from ear to ear.

It took only that one little taste for the milk to be approved and the trunk came back for more. Simon tipped the bucket towards another elephant and then mayhem ensued. The first one butted the others out of the way, pushing them away so he could get more milk. In the ensuing tussle that lasted only a few seconds, the bucket was wrenched out of Simon's hand and the contents spilled on the ground. Immediately all three elephants tried to suck and scoop the sticky, muddy mess off the ground.

"Come out Simon," I urged while the elephants were otherwise occupied. Any second now they could turn on him, take their frustration out on him.

"That's enough for now Simon," I said as he squeezed through the opening and we slid the poles back in place.

Simon smiled and everyone moved closer to pat him on the back, slap hands and brush him down. Everyone was talking and laughing and the relief was palpable; the first step in our new lives with the elephants, and theirs with us, had been successfully taken. We left the elephants to calm down after tipping in a 50 kg sack of cabbage leaves, another of reeds and a third of leaves from fruit and other trees in the game park.

Later that day Simon and I returned with buckets of milk but did not attempt to go back into the enclosure. Elephants in the wild suckle with their mouths from the mother's teats which are situated between the front legs, unlike most other animals whose teats are at the rear. Elephant calves curl their trunks back over their heads to get their mouths onto their mother's teats so getting them to suck milk up with their noses wasn't as easy as it sounded. What we were so patiently trying to achieve was for us to become their surrogate mother and for a bucket of milk and porridge to be their replacement mother's milk.

We made up a very thick mixture of porridge, milk powder and water and split it into two buckets. Pulling the three lowest, horizontal poles out of the doorway, Simon and I squatted down on the ground and held the buckets of milk through the opening. The elephants were used to the smell and voices of me and Simon and this was a far less confrontational situation for them. With Simon holding one bucket and me the other, we waited while the elephants assessed the situation. Smelling, head shaking and small steps forward and then backwards they finally seemed to decide we weren't a threat and came forward to suck the milk and porridge out of the buckets.

Simon and I didn't say a word as long grey noses dropped into the buckets and sucked up milk and porridge with their trunks. It was a slow and noisy business, their trunks didn't have the ability to suck large quantities at once but it was music to our ears: slurping and gurgling, pouring and swallowing. No words were needed; our smiles and shining eyes said it all. From the moment the three baby elephants drained those buckets with their trunks, we had become their surrogate mothers and everything connected with their rearing and handling would get so much easier from then on.

By the sixth day the elephants had calmed down enormously and Simon had given them all names.

"The biggest one I am naming Fanta!" Simon said he'd chosen the name in recognition of the company who were going to be the biggest contributors towards the costs of the elephants' food. The soft drinks company, Delta, had provided years of food for 'Coke,' the big female elephant who had outgrown the Woodlands and so now Simon chose Fanta as a name for this new baby.

The other male elephant, slightly smaller than Fanta, Simon named Mukuvisi, immediately shortened to Muku.

"A long time from now when we are old and tired and Muku is a very big elephant bull, we will be proud for everyone to know that his name tells of his first home: the Mukuvisi Woodlands."

The little female, already our trouble maker, Simon christened Rundi, in memory of the place of her birth. The Lundi River flows into the Gonarezhou National Park where Rundi had come from. By naming her Rundi, Simon said no one would ever forget her real home or how and where she had started her life before people got involved.

TWO

....

It wasn't long before Rundi, Muku and Fanta were all drinking thick milk and porridge out of buckets and had calmed down significantly. Simon had worked tirelessly with them for almost a week and was covered in scratches and bruises from too many close encounters. Getting the elephants to drink from buckets was no mean feat, even from a biological point of view. Studies of elephants in the wild showed young calves kneeling down at water holes and drinking with their mouths, only starting to use their trunks when they were three or four months old, and here we were trying to persuade them to drink out of buckets! Over time their ability to suck and hold liquid in their trunks improved resulting in not so much getting spilt before it was squirted into their mouths. If our three elephants had been in the wild, it was very likely that Rundi, younger and smaller than the others, would probably not have been proficient with her trunk yet. This explained a lot of our problems: she was hungry a lot of the time.

We had learnt a lot in that first week: what they liked to eat, traits of their behaviour including dominance and aggression and, from Rundi, we had learnt about hand sucking. Hand sucking had started when Simon filled his hand with soggy bread and then shoved his fist into Rundi's mouth to make sure she got the food. At first Simon would just put the food in her mouth and then pull his hand out but as Rundi got a taste for the milky bread she would grab Simon's arm, guide his hand into her mouth and start sucking it. When she started doing it to me too, even at times when I didn't have anything to give her, it dawned on me that this wasn't just looking for food, it was probably giving Rundi some comfort, just like suckling on her mother's teat might do.

Once Simon and I were confident that the elephants were calm enough to be handled it was time to start looking at their wounds properly. Until then I'd had to be content with the odd spray of antiseptic onto a wound before beating a hasty retreat. The elephants still hadn't been let out of the circular stockade in the boma but had got used to us going in and out with milk and food, to clean their water and remove manure from their bedding. We pulled a couple of the lowest horizontal poles out of the doorway of the enclosure, watched by Oscar and Ray who were standing by in case we needed help. Ray, always the worrier, asked for the umpteenth time:

"Are you sure it's safe?"

Simon and I exchanged smiles and raised eyebrows.

"They're ready!" Simon said as he went first, bending down, crawling under the poles and wriggling his way into the stockade, closely followed by me. I didn't think we would have a problem as long as there was plenty of food on hand.

I was wrong!

To reduce competition and shoving, we were already mixing up three buckets of milk and porridge so that each elephant got their full share and Oscar passed these in to us as soon as we were ready. The idea was that after the elephants had drunk their milk and were calm and satisfied, I'd have a look at their wounds and see what sort of treatment was going to be needed. Simon took one bucket in each hand for the two male elephants and I took the third bucket for Rundi.

Everything started off so well: Rundi came to me, the two males went to Simon and for a few minutes the only sound was loud, contended slurping. Things started to go wrong as soon as Fanta emptied his bucket. Without hesitating Fanta moved across, dropped his trunk into Rundi's bucket, pushing her out of the way with one hefty thump of his backside. Before we knew what was happening Simon and I found ourselves caught in between two angry elephants. In a few seconds Fanta had drained Rundi's milk bucket and she reacted by smashing her head into him; he reciprocated and then they went at each other repeatedly, heads crashing into bodies while we were helplessly stuck in the middle.

We went down like a pack of cards; first me, then one bucket, then Simon and two more buckets. A great commotion ensued with elephants trumpeting, pushing and shoving, clouds of dust everywhere and Oscar and Ray shouting at us to get out before we were trampled. Lying flat on the ground on my stomach, sand, leaves and grit in my mouth and eyes, I reached out for Oscar's hands and he dragged me out unceremoniously by one arm, not letting go until I was safely under the poles and out of reach of the elephants. Simon's rescue was similarly speedy and brutal.

The two of us must have looked a sight sitting side by side on the ground, covered in dirt and dust, scratches and grazes. We were shaken and shocked but unhurt; in fact the most painful part of the whole escapade had been the high speed wrenching by Oscar to get me out of there! It was only when we saw the state of the three retrieved milk buckets that we realised our near miss. One bucket was folded in half like a sandwich, the other two dented and battered.

"Enough for today?" I asked.

Simon nodded.

Neither of us dared look at Ray; we could almost hear him saying: I told you so!

"We'll try again tomorrow when they've calmed down," I said, picking up the squashed bucket and trying to save face by saying I was off to get a new bucket.

The next day we tried again. Double milk and porridge rations given in three buckets first and when this was finished and all the buckets had been removed, Simon and I went into the stockade. Simon diverted attention with horse cubes, tomatoes and cabbage leaves while I had a close look at the elephants. They were all covered in wounds, particularly around their eyes, heads and on their legs. The wounds around their eyes were mostly bruises which they must have got from bashing into poles and the walls of crates. All three elephants had soft, puffy swellings around their eyes and a few open cuts, some of which had started to heal on their own.

The wounds around the elephants' feet were rope burns from where their legs had been tied together when they were first captured and lifted onto poles, pallets and crates. Most of these sores were much deeper than the others and not healing up; many had gone septic with pus oozing out in beads. These wounds had attracted flies which clustered around the sores; before we knew it, we'd have to deal with maggots too: nature's cleaners of rotten flesh but something I wasn't good with.

In one pocket of my grey dust jacket I had antiseptic wound spray in an aerosol canister, the lid off, ready to be used immediately. In the same pocket I had a couple of quarters of an apple, just in case I needed to hand out a hurried bribe. In my other pocket I had a plastic bag with wads of wet cotton wool, already pre-soaked with disinfectant, ready to dab on wounds. I also had a plastic bottle of antibiotic wound powder which I knew worked wonders on cuts and sores.

As quickly and unobtrusively as I could, I squirted as many open wounds as I could reach with the wound spray; wiped away pus with cotton wool swabs and puffed the pale yellow antibiotic powder into open sores. Neither Fanta nor Muku took any notice of my ministrations;

they were far more interested in the cubes and vegetables that Simon was offering them.

Rundi was a different matter altogether. She swung around with ears spread and trunk tucked under her chest the moment I touched one of the sores on her leg. I immediately stopped and held out a piece of apple from my pocket, relieved that I'd been prepared and had anticipated another close encounter with her. Rundi sniffed the apple before snatching it from my hand. I waited while she ate it and offered her another piece which was eagerly taken. When there was no apple left Rundi took my hand in her trunk and pulled it up into her mouth. Her suckling instinct was very strong and I stood still while her enormous pink tongue gripped my hand and she sucked mightily. Rundi sucked harder when I tried to pull my hand out of her mouth and I turned my head at the sound of Simon's chuckling.

"Take over in here Simon!"

Simon scattered cubes and vegetables on the ground for Fanta and Muku before coming over and slipping his hand into Rundi's mouth while I removed mine. At first very unnerving, we now both agreed that this hand sucking was an extension of suckling; just as a dairy calf sucks on your fingers when it's being taught to drink from a bucket or bottle.

My hands covered in Rundi's saliva I gently pushed pus out of the rope burns that had turned into suppurating sores on her legs, covered them with antiseptic wound spray and puffed in plenty of antibiotic powder. Rundi wasn't at all keen on the cold, wet, cotton wool swabs and reversed a few steps as I tried to use them to clean the sores. It was a bit disconcerting having my head a few centimetres away from her huge feet so I worked as fast as I could, continually listening for the slurping sounds of her sucking on Simon's hand. There wasn't much that could be done about the bruises and swellings around her eyes but now that the elephants had quietened down enough to be touched, it would be much easier to treat their wounds on a daily basis.

A week and a day had passed since the elephants' arrival and the time had come to let them out of the circular stockade and into the main part of the boma. In the eight days they had been with us they had started to get used to the smell and sound of people; the noise of traffic and the taste of highveld vegetation. The boma was not only a place for familiarisation but also one of quarantine and so far the elephants showed no signs of disease.

"OK?" I whispered.

Simon nodded, giving me the thumbs-up sign indicating he was ready. We had discussed the plan in advance and both knew what to do. We pulled out the poles forming the gate of their circular stockade and waited for them to come out into the half acre paddock. This section of the boma was surrounded by a four metre high wire mesh fence covered with thatching grass so the animals couldn't see out and topped with barbed wire. Surprisingly Rundi was first; she came jauntily to the gateway, put one foot out and then looked up. Instantly her eyes darted wildly, ears spread and trunk got tucked under her chin as she hastily reversed back into the safe and familiar stockade. The next grey face to appear at the gateway was that of Fanta. He was cautious, raising his trunk he tested the air for new smells outside the circular stockade that had been home for eight days. Fanta stood smelling and looking for some minutes but then he too reversed back into the stockade.

"Let's try the food Simon," I suggested and he tipped out a sack of cabbage leaves about ten metres from the doorway. The response was instant.

Muku took a step through the gateway, the smell of cabbage leaves clearly too much of a temptation. He made straight for the food and started on the sweet, crunchy cabbage leaves. Within seconds he was joined by Fanta who had a voracious appetite and then only Rundi was left inside the stockade. Eventually she approached the gateway, her trunk raised. Rundi sniffed in all directions, shook her head causing her ears to slap noisily against her back and then stepped cautiously out of the circular stockade. Rundi moved over to the dwindling pile of cabbage leaves and joined in the feeding and as soon as she was busy I signalled to Simon who quickly lined up the poles and threaded them back across the gateway closing off the stockade. Oscar, Ray and Joçam had been waiting out of sight and they quickly moved in and made a start on cleaning out the stockade. Simon stayed with the elephants, keeping them calm and talking to them and when the cabbage leaves were finished, the elephants began to explore the boma paddock.

"Milk's ready Simon," I said putting one very full bucket of thick milk and porridge down on the ground for him to give to the two males while I kept a half full one for Rundi. Simon held one full bucket for Muku and Fanta to share while I took the other half full bucket and led Rundi a little distance away. She was still suspicious of me but her new love for the milk was obviously overpowering as she immediately put her trunk into the bucket and began sucking up milk and pouring it into her mouth. She soon cleaned up the thick, sweet mixture and when there wasn't even a drop left in the bucket Rundi took my hand in her trunk and pushed it into her mouth, sucking strongly.

Rundi wasn't the only one with this strong suckling instinct and Simon and I laughed as Muku wandered over to us and began sucking the edge of Rundi's ear and Fanta joined in, sucking Simon's hand. When the elephants' interest in hand and ear sucking waned, Simon and I led the three calves to the nearby hosepipe, switched on the tap and gave the elephants their first really good wash. All three obviously loved the water and stood with ears spread and trunks up as Simon sprayed them for almost half an hour. I took the opportunity to clean their wounds, push pus out of sores and got thoroughly soaked in the process. The elephants seemed to barely notice my ministrations as they were completely absorbed in their shower.

Later, their boma clean, new hay stacked up in great piles, scrubbed water troughs, raked ground and wetted poles, we opened the gates and led the three contented calves back into the stockade. They sniffed around for a few minutes and then, something usually only seen in younger elephants, collapsed on their sides in the deep hay and fell asleep. For the first time I felt my unspoken doubts and conflicted anguish of what was happening to these elephants receding; perhaps they could adjust to man's interference and have a good life even after the loss of their herd?

"Hi Cathy, are they ready yet?" asked the voice on the phone.

It was our vet, Morna Knottenbelt, calling to find out if she could come and look over the new elephants. Morna knew only too well how critical the one-to-one bonding with the elephants was in these early days and had been waiting for me to give her the go ahead to visit and check the animals over.

"Yes I think so Morna, but they are still quite pushy, so prepare yourself!"

Quite pushy was an understatement but Morna was tough and I knew she didn't expect tame and angelic elephants so soon after their traumatic capture and journey. We arranged a time for her visit.

The elephants had been with us almost a fortnight and their routine was well established. Let out into the small paddock at seven in the morning, they ate grass and leaves in the enclosure, rubbed against trees and rolled in the sand. Milk and porridge in buckets was given at ten followed by sacks full of cabbages, reeds and a few handfuls of high protein pellets which we all called 'cubes' or 'horse cubes.' A good long shower from the hosepipe was given mid morning and the elephants would take themselves off for a sleep, usually in the heat of the day. They were only closed into the smaller circular stockade at night although the gateway door was left open all day so they could go and sleep in their hay piles whenever they wanted to.

Morna arrived just before ten, as arranged, and by the time she had her dust coat and boots on, the morning milk was ready and we all went in together. While Simon and I held buckets of milk and porridge and got dribbled on, Morna had a good look at the now almost healed wounds. She measured them against a stick to get their heights and allowed her hand to be sucked so that she could feel their teeth and look at their eyes.

"Well?" I asked.

"They look excellent, you've done well."

"Simon deserves all the credit," I said and he beamed at the praise.

"You need to watch this little one though," Morna said, stroking and patting Rundi; "she's a lot smaller and younger than the others and needs quite a bit of feeding up." Morna suggested a few more tomatoes be included in the diet to increase vitamin C intake and, if we could afford it, suggested we give Rundi milk and porridge twice a day.

"Have they met Coke yet?" Morna asked.

"No, that's on the cards for later in the week."

Morna smiled and raised her eyebrows: "Good luck with that one!" she said.

"Thanks! I think we'll need it!"

The day came for the big meeting and it was undoubtedly going to be another milestone for the elephants, and for us. We were planning to walk the baby elephants out of the boma and into the Mukuvisi game park. Here they would meet Coke, an elephant much bigger and older than them, but they would also come across a bad tempered white rhino we called Charlie Brown as well as zebra, tsessebe, wildebeest, impala, eland and all the other inhabitants of the 109 hectare game park.

At seven the next morning we unlocked that gates that led out of the boma and into the game park.

"Ready?" I asked.

Simon responded with a smile but I think we were both as nervous and anxious as each other. I pushed the big, four metre high gates open. We had decided to introduce the three elephants to the park very early in the morning before any tourists or spectators were around. With Simon in the lead, the three elephants tramped out in single file and I took up the rear.

For the first time I got a chance to really look at the elephants, out in the bush, where they should be, and realised how little I knew. With the view of only a grey backside in front of me I looked at the tail: hard and rounded, flattened near the tip with long, thick, bristly black hairs hanging down. Unconsciously I rubbed my wrist and for a moment felt ashamed. How many times as a youngster had I worn elephant hair bangles? They were all the rage at times in my youth, eight or ten tough, smooth, black strands knotted together and made into a bangle. I had the urge to reach out and touch the elephant tail hairs now, just a few centimetres in front of me, but I knew what they felt like and it was an emotional revelation to be seeing them where they should be: attached to a living breathing elephant's tail!

Then I looked at the big feet of the elephant walking in front of me. Round and soft looking, the feet are covered with a layer of thick subcutaneous cushioning and cartilage which acts as a shock absorber, the soles spreading out when the elephant puts its foot down and shrinking when lifted up. It was this amazing, soft cushioning that apparently allowed the elephant to walk without making a noise. Thinking of the amazing structure of the elephants' feet reminded me of those outrageous cork wedge heels that we used to wear when we were teenagers. With the elephant so near to me I couldn't help but notice how they walked: the heel touching the ground first, sole splaying out before the front of the foot and toes made contact with the soil, lifting up last. For a second I stood still, closed my eyes and listened: a very soft scuffing sound was the only noise I could hear from three elephants walking less a metre in front of me.

We walked through the now dry Chiraura river bed. It was September, six months since it had rained and the last signs of green in the thick tussocks of grass that grew along the river bank and in the marshy wetland had gone. In the vlei the grass was bleached, scratchy and dry and we passed occasional patches where sweet grass grew, all of which had been grazed down to the dust. We walked on a well trodden, narrow path in single file and headed towards a grove of wild fruit trees on the far side of the vlei. Neither Coke, the big four-year-old elephant, nor Charlie Brown, the temperamental white rhino, were in sight. Making good progress, it only took us fifteen minutes to get to the grove of Muhacha trees (*Parinari curatellifolia*). Simon and I sat on an anthill and watched the elephants browse on leaves and gorge themselves on the fallen fruits. This was their first really good feed since their arrival at the Woodlands and for a change there was no limit to the amount of food available to them. They were familiar with the muhachas as we had been cutting branches and collecting fruits from these trees every day and taking them to the elephants in the boma.

Fanta and Muku seemed totally unconcerned at being out in a new environment without visible thatched fences, poles or gates and they stuffed food into their mouths without pause. Rundi however, was clearly alert and nervous. She kept testing the air for new scents, her little trunk lifted and smelling deeply in all directions. She continually checked where Simon was and didn't move more than a few metres away from him. Every few minutes she stopped eating and moved across to Simon, touching his face, head and neck with the tip of her trunk.

"I am her Mummy," Simon said and it certainly seemed that Simon had been accepted by Rundi as a surrogate mother. At that stage I also began to think that I was starting to be accepted as a part of the elephants' extended family. Now that they had stopped fighting us and calmed down they were the most gentle and loving creatures, always touching, rubbing and nuzzling us. They put as much passion into loving us as they had into fighting us.

We sat for about an hour before wending our way slowly back to the boma in the same single file line we had used in the morning with me bringing up the rear. It had been an uneventful excursion; we had met no other animals which was a relief as it would have been a disaster if the elephants had been frightened on their first day out. Back in the boma with the gates locked behind us, it wasn't too long before the mid morning buckets of milk and porridge arrived. Long deep sucks, loud slurping and sticky trunks followed and then all three lay down on their sides and fell asleep. Simon and I went off to get a cold drink, congratulating ourselves on achieving another milestone: the first excursion into the wild.

Our daily walks with the elephants went very well for the next few days with no unexpected meetings or scares and the three elephants soon knew the route well and became more adventurous. They would leave our well trodden path; pluck a clump of grass or a few stems of a plant before ambling back in line as we headed towards the tree line. Then one morning I arrived late and found that Simon hadn't set out on the elephant walk yet.

"Is something wrong?" I asked

"It's Coke," Simon said, "she won't go away."

Simon and I walked to the gates and there was Coke, waiting outside the boma, sniffing the thatched fence very closely. She could obviously smell something; was it the three baby elephants? We didn't know but I suspected it was when Coke started her low deep rumbling noise.

"Let me go and get cubes," Simon said, this was the treat that the elephants couldn't resist. We weren't going to try and chase Coke away but wanted to be prepared in case there were any problems.

"Got them?" I asked when he returned.

Simon nodded, patting the bulging pocket of his green overalls. I opened the gates, hoping for a slow and gentle exit but there was nothing cautious about our departure; there couldn't be with three elephants pushing and shoving to get out, obviously eager to head to the fruit trees and start feeding. Coke bellowed the moment we stepped out of the boma gates, perhaps she thought we were going to chase her away, perhaps Simon had been chasing her away every day, but we ignored her and she calmed down almost immediately and then, to my delight, she just quietly took up the back of the line!

The three babies always walked in single file; Rundi usually took the lead with Muku in the middle and Fanta at the back. To our amazement none of the babies took any notice of Coke at all, they just kept walking on their familiar path across the vlei. Not so for Coke though, she was clearly intrigued. Coke stayed at the back of the line but her trunk never stopped sniffing and gently touching the elephant in front of her until we reached our first stopping place. Simon and I sat on our usual anthill in the now well trodden feeding place under the Muhacha trees. The babies started feeding straight away, plucking leaves off branches and stuffing them into their mouths. While they ate Coke conducted a thorough investigation of the three elephants: she sniffed them from top to bottom, one at a time, gently touching their faces, mouths, backs and genitals. First she would sniff deeply and then curl her trunk up to her own mouth and exhale, blowing the smell of the calves into her mouth. Elephants clearly knew how to taste smells I thought!

Of the three calves, Muku was the one most interested in Coke. He fed voraciously but every now and again, in mid chew, would put his trunk up and smell Coke. After about fifteen minutes Simon and I had a whispered conversation

"Let's move back," I suggested, keen to see if Coke would take a matriarchal role the way elephants in the wild do. Would she protect the three young calves if they became distressed; would they turn to her to take the lead?

"Not too far," Simon said, a worried look on his face.

"Just to there," I said, pointing to a thicket of trees about fifty metres away.

Very slowly and quietly we got up and left the anthill, making our way to the suggested hiding place. We could see the elephants from our new position but they couldn't see us.

Rundi noticed our absence first. When we'd been gone for about three minutes, she began scenting the air all around her, lifting her trunk and sniffing deeply but it was to no avail as I had deliberately chosen our concealment downwind of them. A few more minutes passed and Rundi began to show signs of agitation. Again and again she issued her low rumbling call and sniffed the air. We watched in fascination at the behaviour of Muku. He walked across to Coke, lifted his trunk and laid it towards her shoulder, opened his mouth and began sucking the edge of Coke's ear! She looked enormous next to Muku who had to stretch to reach her ear. I stifled a laugh when I saw Coke's eyes widen as Muku sucked lustily on her ear. At first she tried to pull away but Muku was having none of it and wouldn't leave her alone. Coke gave in and stood still, smelling Muku and touching him with the tip of her trunk while he dribbled and sucked on her ear.

Fanta took no interest at all in our absence, Rundi's calling or Muku's sucking; he just carried on eating. After about ten minutes Rundi let out a great bellow, turned and began walking down the path heading back home; followed in single file by Fanta, Muku and Coke. Muku had changed his place in the line and as they walked he curled his trunk back, obviously smelling Coke: a new friend, new member of the extended family.

Rundi led the procession at a steady pace, walking fast, heading directly for the boma and as they drew further away Simon could bear it no longer.

"Rundi!" he shouted as we came out of hiding. The wind blew his voice and our scent away and he yelled again: "Rundi!"

This time Rundi heard and what followed was pure cartoon comedy. Rundi stopped dead in her tracks and heads thumped into backsides all the way down the line! Rundi swung round, pushed past Fanta, Muku and Coke and ran back to Simon: backside wobbling, ears flapping, trunk swaying. Immediately she reached him Rundi curled her trunk around Simon's arm and pushed his hand into her mouth; you could see her visibly calming down. After a while the line started off again and we left Coke at her stable under the game viewing platform and took the three baby elephants back to the boma for their milk and porridge and mid morning snooze.

The excitement for the day wasn't quite over. After the elephants had drunk their milk and had their mid morning nap, we took them out of the boma again, walking them down to the game viewing platform so that they could be around Coke and start getting used to the noises and smells associated with visitors game viewing. Everything seemed fine between the elephants until Rundi and Muku went to investigate Coke's stable under the platform. The big elephant went wild: pinned her ears back, put her trunk down and charged. Muku managed to get out of the way but Rundi wasn't so lucky, only managing to get out of Coke's way after two or three hefty butts and a lot of loud, high pitched trumpeting. Enough was enough! Simon and I rounded up the three calves and beat a hasty retreat back to the boma where a bucket of horse cubes, half a dozen cabbages and a pile of tomatoes soon calmed them down. In the days that followed Coke waited outside the boma gates every morning and accompanied us on the elephant walk but she wasn't happy when the babies came into her territory at the platform and so we didn't force the issue.

As the days passed Rundi, Muku and Fanta went for longer and longer walks as we exposed them to more of the game park, slowly familiarising them with the game fence and boundaries of their new territory. Then came devastating news. National Parks phoned and said that Fanta was to be taken from the Mukuvisi Woodlands and relocated to another game park.

The news came as a big blow, particularly as Fanta had settled down so well, adjusting to his new surroundings and becoming a part of the little elephant herd. Now there was to be another major trauma in his young life and again I found myself questioning the whole issue of hand rearing baby elephants. I tried in vain to argue against the removal and relocation of Fanta but National Parks were adamant that he had to go; one of a pair of baby elephants at Imire Game Park in Wedza had died. The surviving elephant was pining, not eating and becoming aggressive and unmanageable. Fanta was to be relocated to try and save the situation. My anguish was lessened at the knowledge that Fanta was going to Imire where I knew he would be handled with love and care.

Simon had the unenviable task of leading Fanta onto the truck on moving day. He led the elephant up the ramp, luring him with horse cubes, talking quietly to him all the way. When Fanta was in the truck, the tail gate was shut and a tarpaulin tied down over the bars. From under the cover Fanta bellowed and roared. I could still see him as the cover was being fastened, repeatedly bashing his head against the bars on the side of the truck. Tears stung my eyes as I watched Fanta lie down and try and squeeze out sideways. I felt as if I was betraying a trust I had worked so hard to gain. At the bottom of the loading ramp, Rundi and Muku were in a frenzy: trumpeting, rumbling, swinging round in tight circles.

"Tell the driver to start the truck," I called to Simon over the noise of the distressed elephants. I could hardly bear the anguish.

"What?" Simon shouted back.

I ran to the front of the truck and asked the driver to start the engine. I knew the noise of the vehicle would scare Rundi and Muku but hoped that once Fanta couldn't see and hear the other elephants and hear their bellowing and trumpeting he may also calm down.

The idea worked. The engine roared, Rundi bellowed once before turning and running away, closely followed by Muku. The vibrations of the truck helped to calm Fanta; his eyes widened and he lifted his head, trunk down. Within a couple of minutes the little elephant stood quietly while the tying down of the tarpaulin was completed and then the truck was ready to go. I gave the driver an envelope containing all the information about Fanta that would be needed by the Travers family at Imire and slowly the vehicle set off. Simon sniffed loudly, wiped his nose on his sleeve and went away to find Rundi and Muku. Raymond stood next to me, raised his hand and said softly:

"Goodbye my friend, we won't see you here anymore. Goodbye Fanta."

THREE

....

The departure of Fanta left Rundi and Muku clearly unsettled; they became noticeably more nervous and aggressive. Whenever Rundi heard a vehicle, even in the distance, she would spread her ears and charge wildly at whatever was in her path. Muku would tuck his trunk under his chin, put his tail and ears out and run away trumpeting and defecating. We needed to calm them down as quickly as possible and reinforcing their routine was the best way to do that: long walks in the game area accompanied by Coke and Simon; milk and porridge at ten in the morning, as much food as they wanted in the boma and as few disruptions to their days as possible.

With less competition for food once Fanta had departed, Rundi got a better share of the fruit and vegetables than before. She was still much smaller than Muku, her pelvic bones protruding and pronounced. Once she'd got used to being touched and handled I was able to compare her trunk with Muku's and it was much thinner and floppier, the muscles seemed under-developed. Rundi often dropped food and didn't seem to have the strength to hold things firmly with her trunk. Because the muscles in her trunk were weak, it was longer and less compact than Muku's; it kept getting in the way of her feet and she also took longer to suck up milk from a bucket.

Getting Rundi stronger and healthier became my top priority after the relocation of Fanta. Working with the vet and the Government Veterinary Department we tried other milk formula combinations to try and improve the condition of the elephants. Fresh cow's milk was used instead of milk powder but stopped after a few days when the elephants got diarrhoea; the consensus was that the fat content was too high. Next we tried goat's milk which didn't upset their stomachs but we couldn't get enough of it to meet the elephants' daily requirements and so we returned to the milk powder but increased the quantity in the mixture. At the same time we began putting tree branches and small logs on the ground in the boma for the elephants and these helped them improve the use of their trunks. Rundi's trunk gradually gained strength from constantly picking up branches and we soon noticed that she wasn't dropping as much food as before and was beginning to put on weight too.

Despite the improvement in her feeding capability and their calm daily routines, Rundi was still more agitated than Muku and her aggressive charging continued. This was worrying because it wouldn't be long before they were going to be let out into the game park full time. The main function of the Mukuvisi Woodlands was conservation education and we regularly took groups of school children into the game park. The last thing we wanted was screaming children being chased by an angry elephant or even worse, for someone to get hurt by an elephant. I spent a long time watching her and saw that a pattern of behaviour had begun to develop.

Whenever someone came near the elephants, if Rundi wasn't getting all the attention, she would spread her ears and charge the visitor. In response Simon would immediately put his hand in his pocket and give Rundi some cubes, stopping her in mid charge.

Aha ! That's it, I thought. Rundi has learnt that bad behavior resulted in cubes and Simon was inadvertently rewarding her for charging.

"Simon, you mustn't feed her!" I said one day after witnessing Rundi's ear flapping, dusty charging trick being played twice.

"But she's going to knock someone down," Simon replied, giving me an impromptu little pantomime of what such an event may look like.

"You're rewarding her for being naughty," I said but the look on Simon's face told me he didn't understand. "She's bluffing! You mustn't give her cubes for charging at people."

"Bluffing?" He still looked confused.

"Yes, you know, pretending! Rundi just wants all the attention and she knows that every time she charges you're going to give her cubes. She won't knock anyone down Simon; she'll stop at the last minute."

"Aaah no!" Simon laughed, shaking his head in disbelief.

"OK! Let's try it and see," I responded, bravely or foolishly!

With Simon watching from a distance I went into the boma and called out to Muku. Both elephants lifted their trunks to scent me.

"Come Muku!" I called again. He swayed his trunk from side to side, shook his head slowly, ears slapping against his back, rumbled and walked towards me. I stroked Muku and put my hand in his mouth and he rumbled contentedly.

Out of the corner of my eye I saw Rundi spreading her ears and I knew it was about to happen!

Ears out, trunk tucked under, Rundi charged straight at me. I pushed Muku away, put my hands on my hips in an attempt to look a little wider and more imposing and stood quite still! I could feel my heart thumping and swallowed anxiously when Rundi stopped less than a metre from me. A spurt of dust rose up as she stopped; her ears quivered a little before dropping back against her back and then Rundi lifted her trunk, touched my face and hair and let out a gentle rumble. It was over! I wasn't going to run away, Simon wasn't going to give her any cubes. I'd called the little elephant's bluff and it had worked, this time!

The more time I spent with Rundi and Muku, the more fascinated

I became with elephants. On a short trip to a wilderness area I was enthralled to watch wild elephants and particularly the interactions that went on between mothers and calves, and other females and calves in a small herd. In the wild elephant mothers are extremely protective of their young so it wasn't easy to see what was going on to try and get some ideas on how to raise Rundi and Muku as close to naturally as possible. As soon as a young elephant came into view, someone in the herd would rumble and move in front of the calf, to shield and protect it.

It was the rumbling sound they made that was one very common factor between Rundi and Muku and elephants in the wild. The rumbling consisted of a low throaty noise that sounded almost like purring, starting with a k sound: 'krrrrrr' and was usually made with the trunk held slightly away from the mouth. Rundi and Muku would rumble when someone they recognized arrived; when they were out in the bush feeding and lost sight of each other and generally when they were apparently contended. Every now and again the rumble would change in pitch, becoming deeper and louder and then it seemed to be being used as a warning. I soon got to know the difference between the welcoming rumble and the warning one and over time practised imitating the welcoming 'hello, everything's OK' rumble and always used it when I saw the elephants.

A few days after Rundi and I had the mock charge showdown a letter arrived, post marked Wedza. I turned it over a couple of times before I opened it, sure it was going to be news about Fanta. Please let him be alive, I thought as I took the sheet of paper out of the envelope. A lively letterhead set the tone with sketches of sable and kudu along the top and giraffe, hippo, zebra, wildebeest and impala down the left hand side. My spirits lifted even more when I read the letter:

"Just a quick note to let you know that your little elephant has settled down very well at Imire and seems to be quite content.

We are still feeding him milk with Pro Nutro every lunch time and he goes walking every morning and afternoon. He gets along famously with our little female and they have a lovely mud bath together every afternoon.

We are taking very good care of him so please don't worry about him too much."

It was an enormous relief to know that Fanta was alive and thriving and that Rundi and Muku were also settling down well again. As the weeks went by the characters of the elephants became more defined. Muku was a softy, he always backed down when there was trouble and sucked on the nearest elephant ear or human hand. He was never pushy or aggressive and always followed Rundi or Coke's lead. Rundi was completely the opposite. She was smaller, shorter and lighter in weight than Muku but she was the one in charge, her matriarchal instincts were already at the forefront. Rundi was short tempered and pushy. She often shoved Muku out of the way or crashed into him if he got in her way. She was the one to choose which route to take on their daily walks and always took the lead. Perhaps because of her repeated bumping and crashing into Muku, we noticed that Rundi had a small lump on her hip. Over the weeks it got bigger and was soon the size of an orange. It was obviously an abscess and I wondered if this was what had been making Rundi bad tempered and pushy. It was time for intervention.

Morna came and gave Rundi a long acting antibiotic, no easy task because even though Rundi's skin was thick her senses weren't and a few bent needles were the inevitable result before success was achieved. The antibiotic didn't stop the lump from growing and we watched the abscess get bigger and bigger until finally the skin cracked under the pressure welling up from underneath. It was time to phone Morna again.

"We're going to have to lance it," Morna announced as she sterilized her scalpel when she came the next morning. "Hold her still now!"

As usual we had planned everything around milk and porridge time. Holding an elephant still is no easy task and I had five men helping me, a tin of horse cubes and bucket of milk and porridge on hand. With a steady hand and very firm pressure Morna sliced through the cracked, peeling skin on the abscess on Rundi's back.

We all gasped at the mass of thick yellow pus that immediately began oozing out of the cut. Amazingly Rundi didn't even flinch; she was intent on sucking the last drops of milk out of the bucket. Because of the high position of the abscess on Rundi's hip the pus wasn't going to be able to drain on its own and would have to be squeezed out. Morna began the process; it needed both hands, one on either side of the abscess and considerable pressure to force the pus up from the bottom of the wound.

After a little while Morna stood back to let one of the men take over while she busied herself with a very large syringe. By this time Rundi was getting a little restless and had started to move around quite a lot. We could all see that we weren't going to be able to hold Rundi for much longer. Morna worked quickly, emptying a syringe full of effervescent antiseptic cleanser into the wound. As the liquid bubbled in the deep hole we had opened up, Rundi let out a high pitched trumpeted scream. We couldn't hold her anymore and watched her retreating backside as she went running off to find Muku.

"Here you are Cathy," Morna said, handing me a box of large syringes and two bottles of the cleaning antiseptic solution.

"She'll have to have the abscess syringed out every day, probably for at least a fortnight. Try and get the pus out first though and then flush it clean with water before you syringe it."

Morna laughed at the obviously shocked look on my face and patted me on the shoulder: "Let me know how you get on!"

The flushing and syringing of the abscess wasn't too bad for the first few days but got harder and harder as the cut narrowed and rotten flesh was gradually replaced with new tissue. An elephant's skin is extremely thick and tough so with abscesses, boils and other infected wounds there was a very real risk of the skin closing over, literally closing the pus in. I knew that I had to keep the wound open until all the pus was gone so I changed the treatment to twice a day and often had to force the cut open so that I could flush the abscess. Every day I came out of the boma looking more and more disheveled and harassed as I took the brunt of Rundi's butting and her temper. My hips and thighs were covered with bruises, I was sore all over and my upper arms ached from the exertion of squeezing pus out of a smaller and smaller hole. Amazingly even after ten days there was still pus coming out of the abscess and most days I'd manage to extract at least half cup of the thick yellow pus. I persevered: weekends no longer existed, social life was gone and my days were consumed by elephant ministrations. As the abscess shrunk I took to using the hose pipe at high pressure to force the pus out. This worked well but I always got soaked and every day Rundi bellowed and crashed against me adding more bruises to my collection.

Almost every day I would get knocked to the ground and covered in mud, much to the amusement of my helpers, and every day it got harder to corner Rundi and do the treatment. As soon as she saw us come in the boma gate Rundi would get restless and start backing away. Even the bucket of milk lost its appeal and eventually we had to resort to crowding Rundi into a corner and doing the job as quickly as possible. Christmas was a non event because right through the holidays I went down to the boma morning and evening armed with syringes, antiseptic and whatever fruity treats I had at home to tempt Rundi into standing still for an extra minute. At last, twenty five days later, Morna pronounced Rundi healthy and I breathed a huge sigh of relief that the daily operations could stop. Despite having manhandled her twice a day for nearly a month a very close bond had developed between me and Rundi. Within a day or two of stopping the treatment on her hip she would approach me as soon as I arrived: rumbling, hand sucking, trunk smelling and touching my face and hair closely and leaning against me.

By the beginning of January 1987 Rundi and Muku had been with us for four months. Rundi stood 104 cm at the shoulder and her girth had increased to 161 cm. Muku had a shoulder height of 117 cm and girth of 203 cm. It was time for the baby elephants to come out of the boma full time. In between flushing abscesses and facing down mock charges I had spent many weeks looking for a new home for Coke. The Mukuvisi Woodlands policy on elephants was that we would only be temporary guardians: take them in as orphaned calves straight from culling operations: look after them until they were weaned and calmed down and get them used to being in contact with people. When they were able to care for themselves they would go to a bigger, wilder environment, usually a game farm or ranch. Coke's time to move had come. Leaving Rundi and Muku under the loving and watchful eye of Simon I turned my attention to Coke.

FOUR

....

Re-homing an elephant was not the sort of thing you advertise in the pets section of the local newspaper; if it was perhaps the classified ad would read something like this:

> ELEPHANT: good home wanted for five-year-old, semi-tame African elephant. Weight approx 1,000 kg. Height 2+ metres. Sex Female. Colour grey. Daily dietary requirements:10 litres milk and porridge; 5 kg horse cubes; 60 kg vegetables; 50– 100 kg natural vegetation (leaves, twigs, roots, berries, shrubs, herbs, grass.) Elephant good natured but can be temperamental; sometimes charges; often destroys.

Finding the next home for elephants after the Mukuvisi Woodlands was no easy task. There were always a number of people who said they wanted an elephant but had absolutely no idea about what was involved in caring for it. Coke was long overdue to leave; she had been a great calming influence on the baby elephants, was a wonderful attraction for visitors and school children but she needed more space and we needed more room for the baby elephants.

There had been many problems finding the right home for Coke. Since my searching couldn't be advertised in the press, it was done by word of mouth and finding the right place was a long, slow process.

The first possibility I looked at was totally unsuitable and couldn't have kept a domestic cat let alone an elephant. The property was shabby, run down and neglected and it was obvious that the prospective owner knew nothing about looking after elephants; all he wanted was a tourist attraction to solve his financial problems. This was definitely not my choice of a good home for Coke.

The second candidate had a large estate but with totally inadequate fencing and no resources with which to secure the boundaries. The property was surrounded by smallholder farmers who made their living growing vegetables. I knew that this was not the right place for Coke; it would take her less than a day to find the vegetable plots and she would undoubtedly end up looking down the barrel of a gun.

The third candidate didn't even get visited! He had a ten acre plot on the outskirts of Harare and would never have been able to find the 150 kg of food or 200 litres of water a day that Coke needed.

As the weeks passed I became more and more concerned about finding a new home for Coke. I had the word out at game parks and farms but because she was used to people and mostly tame, Coke needed special circumstances. She had never been in the wild before so needed somewhere where she could still interact with people and be handled but she also needed to be with other elephants. Coke needed a place where she would be safe and free from poachers. One of my biggest fears was that because she had learnt to trust people there was a chance that Coke would walk right up to a poacher. It didn't bear thinking about and strengthened my resolve to find exactly the right place for her. This problem was one that was being repeated with all the elephant calves that were hand reared after being rescued from culling operations, but this wasn't the time to be debating the rights and wrongs of the issue.

At last what sounded like a suitable home for Coke was offered and Ian and I arranged a visit to the large safari ranch in Karoi that weekend. I was fortunate that my husband loved the bush and animals as much as I did because Ian's weekends and after hours for the next two years would undoubtedly be taken over by elephant events. Ian already had a close bond with Coke, having walked with her often in the Woodlands so he was the perfect person to help choose Coke's new home. What we found in Karoi was perfect! The boundary fences were sturdy and well maintained; there was dense vegetation and a good supply of water and best of all there was already a small herd of hand reared elephants on the ranch which were in the care of a full time handler. At night the elephants were paddocked in a stockade made of railway sleepers and during the day they were monitored regularly. The arrangement was made and a moving date set for a month's time. Ian and I were both sad that Coke was going but we knew we had found the right home for her and that it was time for her to move on. Ian put his finger on it when he wrote:

"Coke was a big girl and extremely heavy and powerful. She didn't know her own strength but a little push from her sent you flying. She never intended to hurt anybody but one had to be aware of her strength and respect her."

I went into a flurry of activity. Getting Coke out of the game park was going to have to be a very carefully planned operation. Coke wasn't good with vehicles under any circumstances. It was the policy of the Mukuvisi to use vehicles as little as possible in the game area so as to cause the least disturbance to flora and fauna but there were times it was unavoidable. On the rare occasions when we took a vehicle into the park we inevitably met up with Coke. As soon as she saw the vehicle Coke would spread her ears, lift her trunk for a quick smell and then there was no stopping her. With ears spread, tail out and leaving a trail of dung, Coke would race off in the opposite direction. It was impossible not to laugh at her on these occasions; she ran at a speed amazing for her bulk and the skin on her backside wobbled and shook making it look as if she was wearing baggy trousers! When she was well out of the way of the vehicle, Coke would stop and turn round, stare, do a couple of half-hearted mock charges in the vague direction of the threat and then disappear into the bush.

Coke had been hand reared at the Mukuvisi and her most sought after treat was horse cubes. She had long since been weaned off the bucket but would easily dispose of ten litres of milk and porridge whenever it was offered: a very handy bribe in difficult situations. Coke would hang around the game viewing platform area at times of the day when food was regularly put out for her: cubes, vegetables and fruit. If she wandered off and we needed her to come back to her stable under the platform all we had to do was bang the bottom of a small tin dustbin and she would come tromping back, knowing that horse cubes would be waiting.

About a week before she was due to leave, I arranged for a crate to be delivered to the game park and left open near the platform.

"You want Coke to go already?" Oscar asked me that evening as we stood on the platform and looked down on the massive box. It was a National Parks crate with a steel frame lined with wooden planks on the sides and top, braced and supported all round. It looked to be about three metres high, four or five metres long and wide enough for an elephant to go in but not turn around.

"No, not yet, I just want her to get used to it, the smell and feel of it, and to start going inside it by herself."

"She won't go in by herself," Oscar said, chuckling and shaking his head, looking at me as if I'd gone crazy.

"I think she might if we put her food inside it."

The next morning with Coke watching, I took a couple of handfuls of cubes and laid them in a trail into the crate before retreating to watch. Coke smelt me, the cubes on the ground and then the crate and then immediately started eating the trail. When she got to the doorway of the crate, Coke stopped. She stretched her trunk out, reached into the crate and picked up the cubes she could reach. Further and further she stretched and when she couldn't reach the cubes anymore she very cautiously stepped right into the crate itself, front feet only. She ate the cubes, hastily reversed and then inspected the outside of the crate very thoroughly. She sniffed and touched it from top to bottom but didn't go back inside.

After a few days Coke seemed completely at ease with the crate and was going in and out of it quite naturally without hesitation. When departure day arrived, there wasn't any problem at all. Even with all the extra people milling around waiting to load the crate, Coke simply walked in, and ate the cubes scattered around, standing quite still while the door was closed and the latches secured.

Lifting a box containing an elephant was no easy task but with the aid of poles, ropes and a lot of manpower, the crate was manoeuvred onto the back of the big National Parks truck. The whole process took about half an hour and during the entire time Coke didn't make a sound. Her silence bought a lump to my throat.

Standing in the shade of a large Acacia tree while everything on the truck and crate was checked and secured for the journey, I remembered a day not long before when Coke had given me a big fright. I had been conducting research into the level of tick infestation on the vegetation in the game park. Some ticks, the nymphs, are so small that it's almost impossible to see them with the naked eye so I cut a white bed sheet in half and would walk through the grassland dragging the sheet behind me. Even the minute nymphs could be counted in this way as they looked like peppery specks against the white of the sheet. At the end of a pre-determined section I would stop, count the ticks sticking to the sheet and get a rough idea of the distribution and infestation levels of ticks in the grassland.

It's hard to believe that an elephant standing almost two metres high could be missed, but it was something that happened often with Coke. Lost in thought I was walking through the tall grass dragging my sheet behind me when Coke suddenly appeared right in front of me. Getting a fright I gasped and dropped the sheet. The thin fabric lifted up on a gust of wind and billowed straight at Coke. Then it was her turn to get a fright and her instinctive reaction was to charge: straight at me. When her huge grey bulk was almost on top of me, I could see she wasn't going to stop and shouted at the top of my voice:

"Coke! No!"

The elephant stopped, looked at me, shook her head from side to side, ears slapping noisily against her shoulders and she turned round, heading back into the long grass. With racing pulse and shaking hands I retrieved my sheet and carried on with my survey but after that I always checked where Coke was before I started dragging bed clothes around the vlei.

Now that Coke was leaving the Mukuvisi Woodlands, I realised how much I was going to miss this gentle creature; she had given me lots of scares but also caused me to laugh on so many days. The securing of the crate seemed to be taking a long time and Coke started getting restless. She trumpeted once and I tried to calm her by talking softly to her through the wooden slats. A couple of the Parks men were sitting on top of the crate securing ropes and tightening straps.

"Is she OK?" I asked one of them as the noises from inside increased. They could see Coke quite easily through the gaps between the planks in the roof of the crate.

"She's on her knees and hitting her head against the sides," he said. "Don't worry, it won't be long now, we're nearly finished."

Thankfully the tying down was soon completed and as the truck started up and began to pull away, we saw Coke's trunk come out of the top of the crate. We knew she must have got back onto her feet and that was the last sight we had: the tip of her trunk smelling for the last time the place where she had spent the first few years of her life. Knowing that Coke was going to be with other elephants and become part of a herd made my pain and sense of loss easier to bear.

The day after Coke left, Rundi and Muku had their buckets of milk and porridge at the platform. This was a first for them because although they had by then been with us for four months, they had always been given their milk in the boma. Everything was fine until their buckets were empty and the cubes finished and then Rundi started to panic. She ran to the gate, rumbled loudly, raised her trunk and scented the air in all directions. Muku ambled over and started sucking her ear and for a while the two little elephants just stood at the gate looking quite forlorn and obviously unsure about what to do next. Without the visual boundaries provided by the thatch of the boma walls and with Simon out of sight cleaning their buckets and having his tea, the elephants were lost.

A zebra stallion that had been drinking at the pan in front of the platform came quite close to them, obviously with the intention of cropping some of the lush grass growing on the spillway. Muku went crazy, spread his ears, trumpeted shrilly and mock charged the zebra, turning away just before he reached him. Muku retreated to a safe distance and then repeated the whole performance. It was obvious that the elephants were not ready to be left alone at the platform, not even for the time it took for Simon to have cup of tea and a sandwich. I went in the game gate and immediately Rundi and Muku came running over to me, calming down straight away, touching my face and hair with their trunks and looking for a hand to suck. Raymond came in the game gate soon after pushing a wheelbarrow and then Rundi and Muku followed him everywhere. As he loaded dirty straw into his wheelbarrow they unloaded it, sniffed it and threw it on themselves and on the ground.

"You're not winning over there Ray!"

"I am not winning," he replied smiling, watching the baby elephants unloading all the dirty straw he'd put in the wheelbarrow for the second or third time. Now that Rundi and Muku were going to be spending a lot more time at the platform everyone was going to be able to interact with them, and get used to the elephants helping us with our daily chores.

As the weeks passed, Rundi and Muku became less and less frightened of being left alone and got more adventurous. Their daily routine still consisted of a long early morning walk with Simon, milk and porridge at the platform and then they were left on their own for a little while, alongside a big pile of vegetables sprinkled with cubes as hidden treats. They soon took to sleeping in the space underneath the platform which also served as a stable. In the afternoon Rundi and Muku would walk down the wide path to a small dam where there was muddy water to roll around in and lush vegetation to feed on. At night we still closed Rundi and Muku into the boma, although they were no longer confined to the small central circular stockade. This worked well for a while but before long they started to tear down the thatching grass which covered the fencing and then one day they broke out and I wrote about the encounter in the Woodland Newsletter that went out to all our members:

"A couple of days prior to their release they managed to escape from the boma and gleefully headed towards the kiosk. A group of young children having cold drinks there all hastily got out of the way; one young boy was overheard calling out: 'Hurry! The Monsters are coming!'"

Soon after this we moved Rundi and Muku out of the boma altogether and they began spending their nights in the stable under the platform.

I finally began to feel that the elephants had really settled down when they began to play. Frequent observations were made in the game patrol reports of Rundi and Muku playing: running, pushing, shoving, cavorting and flopping around. Often they would lower their heads, touch their foreheads together and push mightily against each other. This would go on for a long time becoming more invigorated if one elephant gained a little ground. If one of them found and picked up a stick that the other one fancied a great game would ensue with running, pushing, trunk twining and stretching with repeated attempts by one elephant to snatch the item away from the other. Sometimes this game when they both wanted the same object such as a stick, piece of bark, pod or even a strand of lichen, turned into a chasing game and the two would run through the bush, one behind the other, trumpeting squeakily.

One afternoon Beth Taylor and her son Peter went on patrol with a professional hunter. They stopped for a break under some shady trees and Peter recalled what happened:

"The two elephant babies had already gone ahead and were not with us. We had our normal tea and snacks, and still no eles, but on our way back just before coming out into the vlei there was a load of trumpeting behind us. Rundi burst out with Muku charging up behind her, making a hell of a racket. The professional hunter nearly had a fit and explained later that out in the bush where there is a noisy baby elephant, there is going to be a very bad tempered mother not far behind! Luckily in this case it was just an elephant game."

On another occasion Beth and Pete witnessed an amazing game between elephants and tortoises. People were always bringing tortoises to the Woodlands that they had found in unsuitable urban areas and every now and again, when conditions were right and there was plenty of suitable vegetation in the bush, we would mark the tortoises, record their details and release them into the game area. Beth was the expert at this job and after marking the tortoises she would load them into a box and carry them out into the game park, noting where and when she released each one. Whenever she walked in the game area she would kept a special watch for the tortoises, recording where she saw them, how far they had moved from where she released them and what condition they were in. Pete Taylor related the unbelievable encounter he and his Mum witnessed one afternoon between two elephants and two tortoises, the latter probably not standing much taller than the elephants' toenails.

"On one of Mom's tortoise releases there was a big male tortoise that took up a home in the Secret Forest. On one of our patrols we stopped to have a cup of tea and Muku, who was always into everything, found this rather energetic male tortoise busy with a female, making a hell of a noise. Muku found this very interesting and spent a good half an hour rolling the tortoise and playing push ball with it between himself and Rundi As soon as the tortoises tried to get away they were sniffed, kicked and pushed all over the place by the elephants again. To the two little elephants, these walking, noisy rocks were a great toy to play with."

Rundi and Muku settled down well at the platform and before long their lives took on a routine, one of which was Mondays with me; an encounter that sometimes drove me nuts. Every Monday I spent two or three hours collecting fresh samples of faeces from the six predominant species of animals in the game park: zebra, wildebeest, impala, eland, tsessebe and, of course, elephants. Samples were bagged, labelled and sent to the government Veterinary Department for analysis. Scientists looked for worms and eggs in the faeces and in this way we could monitor the fluctuations and build up of parasites such as liver fluke. I would go armed with a pocketful of plastic bags and labels, collect the samples and try to be finished by mid day when the samples were collected.

As soon as I went in the gate by the platform on a Monday morning, Rundi and Muku would raise their trunks, take in a lungful of my scent, rumble their welcome and come plodding over to join me. Before I could do anything Rundi would snatch my hand for a suck and Muku would suck on her ear at the same time: a standard ritual which took place every time I went in the gate. When the greetings, dribble and sucking was over we would set out. The order was always the same: Rundi in front, me in the middle and Muku at the rear.

First I had to locate the animals I needed samples from and either find a fresh sample of newly deposited dung or wait for the animal to oblige. With 109 hectares to cover, two thirds of which was quite thick woodland, Dung Day entailed a fair bit of walking. Rundi and Muku followed me all the way, occasionally diverting from the path to snatch a few leaves or fallen fruits or to throw sand over themselves.

Collecting samples from the wildebeest and impala was easy enough as they almost always used middens, regular bush latrines, and I could just collect some fresh faeces from the top of the pile. The other animals weren't so easy. Muku had a great dislike of the zebra for some strange reason and every time we got anywhere near the herd Muku would spread his ears and rush at them, bellowing and trumpeting and causing the animals to immediately race off into the nearest patch of thick bush. Sometimes Muku's charging caused the zebra to defecate in fright which was good because it gave me the necessary sample! Other times the zebra just ran away and we would have to follow them and then wait to collect a sample. Rundi never gave any trouble on Dung Day, she plodded along just ahead of me, checking all the time that I was nearby. She stopped when I stopped and carefully smelt all the samples that I collected.

Before I started working with elephants I was rather sceptical of the idea that wild animals have personalities but soon changed my mind. Muku was a follower, soft and soppy; he always did what Rundi did, went wherever she went, walked at the back, faithfully plodding along behind her. When Rundi was taking an obvious lead and being the matriarch as elephant females are, Muku would show quite a different side to his personality.

He had a very playful nature; I often thought of it as a sense of humour. Muku would wait until almost all my bags were filled with steaming dung samples and then a trunk would come forward and the bag would be pulled gently out of my hand. At first I panicked, giving him no credit for intelligence, thinking he was going to stuff the bag into his mouth. He wasn't! It seemed that all he wanted to do was carry the bag. What a sight we made. We trudged along with Muku nonchalantly swinging a bag of hot manure from side to side, occasionally lifting his trunk and resting the bag on his head. If I tried to take it away from him, he would do his famous 'baggy pants' run: ears flapping, tail straight out, backside wobbling in its wrinkled loose skin. Muku didn't always carry a bag but when he did I soon discovered that it was best to let him hold it because if I tried to get it off him, it invariably got broken. I usually managed to get my bag of dung back from Muku by detouring to a favourite tree or some lush green grass where he would put the bag down to eat and as soon as he did that I could retrieve it. A few times I would get back with a very flat bag of manure because Muku had stood on it, but no one ever queried where I had found wafer thin sheets of faeces.

One morning I got a call from a young veterinary student at the University. The young man wanted some elephant faeces to analyze and see what parasites he could find. Just back from another agonizingly long winded meeting and with mountains of paperwork to catch up on, I offered a much easier option.

"We already know what parasites there are," I said brusquely, "I've got files full of reports you can come and look at if you want."

The UZ student was nervous and I wasn't being very helpful but that didn't stop him; he was determined to get his samples.

"OK," I agreed when he insisted he had to have his own sample. "When do you want it and how much do you want."

"I'll come at lunch time and could I have 10 kg?"

There was a slight pause on my end of the phone.

"10 kg!" I exclaimed.

There was no response on the other end of the phone.

"10 kg!" I said again, "do you really want that much? I usually collect about a hundred grams for the Veterinary Department. 10 kg is an awful lot."

"Oh yes, I need 10 kg," the young man stuttered before putting the phone down.

When the request was relayed to Oscar, Simon and Ray it was cause for much humour and chit chat. 10 kilos of elephant dung was an awful lot and naturally Simon was relegated to the task.

"Simon's the elephant man," Oscar said chuckling, his shoulders shaking, eyes shining with humour. "He's the man for this job!"

Simon headed down to the game viewing platform with a large empty feed sack, a shovel and wheelbarrow. About half an hour later he returned with his smelly, heavy bounty and arrived at the office door with the wheelbarrow and faeces so fresh that you could almost see the steam rising from it and could most certainly smell it! Simon had got carried away and I couldn't even lift the bag in the wheelbarrow. I didn't tip any out; Simon and I gathered the mouth of the bag together, tied it tightly closed with string and put it in the shade of the big Fig tree outside the office.

I was determined to see the look on the UZ student's face when he came to collect his large bag of elephant manure but as the day wore on no one came for the elephant faeces. When I finally set off home at about 5.30 that evening, the bag was still sitting under the Fig tree, surrounded by flies and emitting a very pungent smell.

The next morning when I got to work Oscar was grinning and could hardly wait to tell me what had happened. Just before the Woodland gates closed at 6 pm a University truck roared in and a young man emerged. Oscar pointed to the Fig tree and watched as the young man struggled to lift the sack into the back of the truck. The student had disturbed scores of flies which swarmed around him in a haze. The bag of dung was dripping wet as moisture oozed out of it and damp stains soiled the student's white dust coat and trousers as he hefted the bag into the back of the truck. The student raised a hand, either in thanks or to brush flies away, Oscar wasn't sure which. The wheels of the University truck spun in the dust, stones kicked out in all directions and the student and his bag of dung were gone. I never heard another word from that student but some weeks later another UZ undergraduate phoned and asked for 10 kg of elephant faeces. After a brief chat he agreed that actually 2 kg would be more than enough and after that regularly collected faeces samples for the University veterinary department.

Then there was the old man and the elephant dung.

"There's someone to see you," Oscar announced from the office doorway.

I looked up, surprised, as I hadn't seen a vehicle drive in and usually people came straight to the office when they arrived.

"Oh! Who is it?"

"He's waiting under the tree for you," Oscar said.

A very elderly man stood in the shade. He was impeccably dressed in a three piece suit, shoes shined till you could see your face in them and he wore a beautiful brown tweed hat. As I approached, the man lifted his hat revealing a very grey head of hair. He offered me his bony, gnarled hand. Once the formal questions and greetings, essential in African culture, were completed we got down to the reason for his visit.

"What can I do for you Sekuru?"

The old man said he wanted a bag of elephant 'doings.' As always, hating to be left out of anything, Oscar was hovering nearby and he broke into a conversation in Shona with the man. A fairly lengthy dialogue ensued which Oscar then translated into just a few words. It seemed that my visitor was a traditional healer and wanted a bag of dry elephant manure to use in his trade. When I asked what he used the elephant dung for, Oscar interrupted and took over the explanation himself, muttering dismissively about smoke and healing powers.

Judging by the look on Oscar's face it was pretty clear that I should abandon the questions.

"No problem," I said to the old man and asked Oscar to give the man a bag and show him where he could collect the dung from our compost heap.

Oscar had suddenly and inexplicably become very off hand and bored with the whole encounter. He shouted over his shoulder for one of the workers to come and take over.

The old healer lifted his hat to me again and went off to get his elephant manure.

"What's going on Oscar?" I asked, confused at his sudden off-hand manner.

"Aaah," he said slowly, scratching his head, "you never know about these people, they have a lot of magic. It is better if I keep away."

Oscar was very wary of the old man and obviously quite uncomfortable round him so I didn't push it. A little later when I saw Oscar going past towards the game viewing platform, I seized the opportunity of being out of Oscar's view and went to where the old man was busy collecting dung. I asked him again to explain how he was going to use the elephant manure. The old healer straightened up, took a spotless handkerchief out of his pocket, wiped his hands and forehead and proceeded to tell me very politely how he used the manure.

He said a few stones would be arranged in a circle on the ground and the elephant manure placed in the centre and ignited. The healer said the smoke contained very special properties and could cure such things as persistent nose bleed. The patient would be made to inhale deeply of the smoke for a few minutes and then the bleeding would stop. He was reluctant to say more so I left him to it but later found out that elephant had dung had many other uses, particularly by midwives. It was apparently used during pregnancy and at the birth to dilate the vagina to enable easy delivery.

There seemed to be no end to the fascinating aspects of everything relating to elephants. With each passing day I realised how incredibly lucky I was to be having this amazing experience, despite all my reservations about the rights and wrongs, the morals and ethics of hand rearing baby elephants.

FIVE

....

Rundi and Muku had been with us for six months; Rundi was eleven and Muku thirteen months old. Rundi was definitely the more dominant of the two elephants, her matriarchal role clearly apparent even at that young age. Whenever I could I spent time observing them and could see that an elaborate set of behaviour patterns had already become established despite the absence of adult elephants. Most noticeable was the constant bonding behaviour that went on between them.

The two elephants spent a lot of time touching each other, often initiated by Muku. With the tip of his trunk Muku would touch Rundi's eye or ear, tail, back or legs. They would often lean against each other and when they slept parts of their bodies would often be touching. Trunk resting was another common tactile behaviour. One elephant would lift its trunk and rest it across the width of the back of the other one, sometimes leaving it there for ten or fifteen minutes. This behaviour was often accompanied by a low rumbling from one or both of the elephants. I couldn't guess what this trunk resting meant or why they did it, or even if it needed to have a reason, but it was a very intimate and moving behaviour to witness.

Then there was what I called: 'what are you eating' behaviour which could have been bonding behaviour, curiosity, learning or was it just greed? One elephant, perhaps Rundi, would pick up something and put it in her mouth. Muku, if he wasn't already eating, would immediately put his trunk up to Rundi's mouth. The half chewed contents in Rundi's mouth would be sniffed and sometimes even pulled out of her mouth if he could get a grip on it. Both the elephants did this a lot, when they were out walking in the bush and when feeding on a pile of vegetables at the platform.

All the vegetables were off cuts, trimmings and surplus stock generously donated by Mike Wilcox who owned Honeydew Farm, three kilometres away. They were an absolute life saver to us; all we had to do was go and collect them and every willing helper with a vehicle was roped in to help because we needed so many vegetables to satisfy the needs and appetites of the elephants. Every day, sometimes twice a day, someone would go to the loading and sorting area at the back of the farm's shop and usually take Simon or Ray to help with the selecting and loading. We would spend ages elbow deep in squishy tomatoes, cabbage leaves and all manner of other vegetables and fruits which were either slightly over ripe, bruised, misshapen or damaged. Sorting and bagging as much as we needed or could carry, these vegetables supplemented the elephants in summer and literally kept them alive in winter.

The 50 kg sacks of vegetables were tipped out at the platform twice a day and were a constant source of scrapping between Rundi and Muku. At first they ate from the top of the pile and as their initial hunger was satisfied, they would fight for the more desirable items. They loved cauliflower florets, beetroot tops, broccoli, cabbage, guavas and mangoes which were eagerly hunted for in the large heap of vegetable off-cuts, accompanied by much pushing, shoving and trumpeting.

With the help of a group of volunteers I had set up a game committee to assist with doing patrols in the game area, monitoring the animals and vegetation and keeping an eye on the elephants. Margaret Matejcic, Sally Claasen, Beth Taylor, Carolyn Dennison and Terry Fallon were the regulars and never failed to put aside half a day at least once a week to come and walk in the game area. Later Chantelle Laing also joined us to help with patrols and collections and this group of willing volunteers and friends became the life blood of everything related to the animals in the 109 hectare game area of the Mukuvisi Woodlands.

Margaret Matejcic was tall and slim, had a fantastic sense of humour and infectious laugh together with an insatiable appetite for adventure. Margaret was always beautifully turned out but never said no to any request I proposed including things that involved mud, slime, urine, blood or manure. Margaret tirelessly raised awareness and money for various projects at the Woodlands. She was our supreme baby carer and would take in any abandoned little creature that came along, rearing it until it could be released or relocated, happily putting up with endless little bottles of milk along with screaming, biting, urinating and all manner of mayhem in her home.

Sally Claasen was a chameleon! On the one hand a stunning woman of the world with a husband in the diplomatic corps, dinner parties and cocktail functions. On the other hand a Mum with a young daughter at home and a burning passion for nature conservation. Sally had boundless energy and an adventurous spirit and always found time for the Woodlands. Sally was up to date on all the latest information on game management and was doing a conservation qualification with a South African University, gladly sharing her knowledge with us along the way. Sally wasn't afraid to get her hands dirty and she bought fun and laughter to every task that needed doing. Sally and Margaret between them gave our little committee a touch of class, bringing glasses and bottles of chilled wine at the end of hot, dirty operations and making huge inroads into our fund raising efforts for a new game fence.

Beth Taylor could best be described as our free spirit committee member she wasn't one for rules and regulations, times and deadlines! Beth drove a bright yellow vw without a licence on the back roads or a

Velosolex on the hard shoulder: nothing would stop her from coming to patrol in the game park. Beth had a warm, kind heart, soft voice and a wicked laugh. Beth loved animals and like Margaret she would take home any little abandoned creature that needed a home or temporary help. Beth often patrolled with her young teenage son Peter, instilling in him a passionate love for the bush and all creatures they came across.

Carolyn Dennison who I immediately called Carol, and got away with it, like me lived across the road from the Woodlands and was a keen bird watcher. Carolyn became a good friend, a very wise and informed adviser, invaluable helper and got on extremely well with all the staff at the Woodlands. Carolyn was a rare breed: a true conservationist as opposed to a bunny hugger. Similar to Sally, Carolyn understood the need for real management when it came to wildlife and conservation and was never afraid of rolling her sleeves up and getting stuck into the dirty jobs that went with it.

Then there was Terry Fallon, the only man amongst us! Terry worked at a tobacco company just down the road from the Mukuvisi Woodlands and had to go past our gates every day. Terry was an avid bird watcher and popped in one day to ask if he could do some bird watching in the Woodlands. As soon as I realised that bird watching could be doubled with patrolling, I pounced on him, and before Terry knew what had happened, he was involved up to his eyes. Immediately recruited onto the game committee, Terry was a bit of a wallflower at our weekly meetings, being the only man present. He seemed to love being out-numbered though, and we loved having him. Terry was enthusiastic about everything and came up with some very wild schemes, particularly after one of his lengthy liquid lunches! Terry popped in every day to see if anything needed doing and invariably there was: collecting vegetables for elephants, arranging bags of slimy tripe for the crocodiles, organizing transport for stock feed, hay and lucerne and like everyone else Terry got involved in the insatiable monster of fund raising.

Everyone in the game committee got involved in collecting vegetables for the elephants and meat for crocodiles, fighting wild fires, clearing noxious water weeds, catching fish, collecting snares, picking up litter and all sorts of other tasks in the game area. We established a roster which ensured that someone was walking in the game area every day and everyone recorded their observations after each patrol. The interaction of the game committee members with the elephants was critical; it helped the elephants get used to being in contact with different people, something that was obviously going to be a part of their lives from now on. It also helped us to observe how the elephants' behaviour changed with different people.

There were a number of people going into the game park on a regular basis. Aside from the game committee members, groups of school children doing educational programmes were escorted by Mike, our education officer, once or twice a week. Visitors and tourists were taken into the game area by voluntary safari guides in small groups every weekend. A fence patrol was done by Leonard or Joçam every morning and Mukuvisi Woodland workers were often doing jobs in the game area, particularly fence repairs. All in all this amounted to quite a number of people coming into contact with the elephants. As a general pattern, Rundi and Muku always went on the game committee patrols, sometimes went on fence patrols but usually got bored or distracted and turned back before long. They never went on the educational tours and sometimes went on the game safaris. Most of the safari guides didn't encourage the elephants to go with them on the group walks because inevitably the elephants dominated everything. It was almost guaranteed that if the safari guide stopped to show people a plant or berry the elephants would push in and proceed to eat the evidence! It was hard to understand why the elephants went on some walks and not others and mostly it wasn't something we could control. In fact quite the opposite; often if you specifically didn't want the elephants around, you couldn't get rid of them.

Carolyn Dennison, a tireless patroller, record keeper and avid bird watcher described going on patrol with the elephants:

"The babies would sniff me first to make sure they knew me and then trot along swinging their floppy little trunks, sniffing the air and giving each other and sometimes me, a bit of a push! Elephants communicate with touch, smell and sound, as their sight is not very good.

What a wonderful and unique experience it was, walking in as near a bush-type habitat as possible near town, with two baby elephants for company. They loved to poke their trunks into nooks and crannies, picking up bits of vegetation and putting it in their mouth to taste to see if it could be eaten; picking up stones and throwing them around, emitting little squeals and trumpeting sounds. They rushed up and down in play, always coming back to me for reassurance and to check I was still around. They liked to have physical contact and would push and lean against me often."

After every game patrol a report was filled in and these records became an invaluable source of information: documenting changes as they happened, giving early warning of impending problems and providing a comprehensive record that became a very useful management tool. Through these reports we built up a picture of what the elephants were eating, which were favoured trees and plants, how long they spent feeding, drinking, resting, dusting themselves and sleeping. It was through the game patrol reports that we were able to quickly pick up on a problem with Rundi.

Towards the end of their seventh month with us, Rundi developed a small lump at the top of her trunk, almost between her eyes where the trunk is quite wide and solid. Watching it daily, the lump grew slowly and when it was about the size of a plum I called the vet.

"I think that's an abscess coming up," Morna said as she felt all round the area at the same time being given the full, once over, sticky trunk inspection from Rundi. While Morna felt and prodded the lump, Rundi's trunk sniffed Morna's face, eyes and delicately touched her hair. We all smiled. This was the Rundi inspection that we all got and it seemed almost insulting to try and stop the elephants from doing this.

"You're going to need to try and draw that abscess up Cathy. Hot and cold compresses twice a day should do it." Morna always told me these things with a lovely glint in her eye; she must have known that applying a hot compress to an elephant was going to be a lot easier said than done.

I prepared to start the treatment that afternoon and while Oscar went back to the kiosk to arrange the hot water, a bowl and cloth, I went to the platform to get a bucket of horse cubes ready. Oscar seemed to be taking ages to arrive and when he did finally appear I dipped the cloth into the bowl of water he'd bought but it was luke warm.

"This isn't nearly hot enough Oscar! It's got to be able to penetrate elephant skin!"

"It was very hot when I got it but I met a woman on the way here and she wanted to know all about the crocodiles."

"OK, it's my turn, I'll go this time."

Throwing the water out I trudged all the way back to the kiosk where the nearest electricity point and source of hot water was. Boiling the kettle I filled the bowl and went back to the platform. By the time I got there, unlocked the gate and Simon had the elephants eating cubes, my bowl of water had cooled down enough to be used.

Soaking the cloth and then pressing it against Rundi's lump, she didn't seem to even notice it and just kept filling her mouth with cubes. So far so good and easier than I thought. The next morning I repeated the process, this time taking a flask of boiling water with me and pressing such a hot cloth against her head that I could hardly bear to hold it. Amazingly Rundi took no notice of the fierce heat of the cloth or of my ministrations to her nose. Twice a day for the next twelve days Rundi got more than her normal share of cubes as I held hot and then cold compresses to the lump on her nose which was now the size of an orange. The abscess looked horrific, the skin had cracked and peeled due to the pressure from within and then, finally, it developed a distinct hot, soft spot.

At last the monster was ready to burst!

The next day Morna arrived; out came a swab, then the sterile scalpel and she expertly sliced open the abscess while Rundi carried on putting cubes in her mouth seemingly completely unconcerned about what was going on. Thick, yellow, foul-smelling pus oozed out of the cut and kept on coming until there was about a cup full of it. Unbelievable, we muttered, where had it all come from; there must have been an enormous cavity below the surface. We squeezed out as much pus as we could, at first Morna and then Simon and I also took turns until at last the flow stopped. Morna filled a 30ml syringe with a mixture of antiseptic and water and squirted it into the hole.

Ouch! Rundi definitely felt that and she immediately bellowed and turned away. Morna hadn't quite finished because there was still the issue of the long acting antibiotic. Morna had a few needles in her pocket this time; she had past experience of the needles bending as she tried to inject the elephants. Morna's job was done and the aftercare was up to me to continue in the days to come.

Twice a day for the next twenty days the abscess had to be squeezed and syringed and the outside sprayed with antiseptic to keep flies and their maggots away. Elephant skin was tough skin to squeeze: hard, wrinkly and with very little flexibility. As the days passed treating Rundi's trunk abscess became an increasingly difficult chore. As soon as Rundi saw me coming she must have known what was going to happen and would get agitated and restless. What should have been a five minute job soon became a half hour task as it took longer and longer to get her to allow the procedure to be undertaken. As the abscess healed and new soft pink flesh began to fill the hole, the treatments were obviously painful and Rundi often bellowed, trumpeted and butted me heavily, often knocking me to the ground and always leaving me bruised and sore. Three weeks later there was nothing left, the hole had closed, the swelling gone and Morna pronounced Rundi fit.

It was easy to underestimate the myriad tasks undertaken by an elephant's trunk: breathing, smelling, carrying, touching, washing and of course lifting food and water into its mouth. After a long time watching Rundi and Muku, the best description I could find for the trunk that it was the equivalent of a human hand. It was sensitive enough to rub the corner of an eye; versatile enough to turn in all directions; flexible enough to pull, wrench and break off items of vegetation; strong enough to carry big branches and lift considerable weights off the ground. After checking on her abscess for the last time, I watched Watching Rundi picking up the last crumbs left from a pile of horse cubes; the tip of her trunk looked just like a hand with a mitten on it: the upper and lower prehensile lips functioning as efficiently as a thumb and finger on a human hand.

Rundi had been a very special elephant from the day she arrived. She was small and thin so getting and keeping her weight up and improving her condition was a constant battle. I had soon discovered that if either of the elephants was going to get sick, it was always Rundi. Morna had started doing research into the mortality of elephant calves that had been orphaned as a result of culling, rescued and translocated to small game parks. The results she was getting were chilling. The year we got Rundi and Muku, ten calves altogether were saved from culling operations and sent to various game parks and farms around the country. Of the ten calves, only four survived the first six months.

Sixty percent mortality was a disturbingly high figure and one that should have raised serious questions about not only the viability but also the morality and ethics of saving elephant calves from culling. Post mortems were conducted on four of the six calves that died and all showed two common factors: massive abscesses, mostly in the lower back and hip region, and malnutrition. A Canadian pathologist investigated the findings and concluded that the abscesses were formed at the time of capture. Calves were caught and manhandled into small wooden crates. They were then sedated with an intra muscular tranquillizer in the upper hind quarters, near the hip. The tranquillizer was injected under extremely difficult circumstances. The operative had to balance on top of the crate and stab a needle in poor light into a wildly thrashing animal. The pathologist assumed that the physical manhandling of the loading, the thrashing of the captured elephant in the crate and then the bumping during transportation over rough bush tracks, caused lacerations and bruises which later went septic and developed into abscesses. The malnutrition which was the second cause of the high mortality was self explanatory. Taking unweaned, wild animals from their mothers, their herds and their habitat was an enormously traumatic and stressful event. The calves needed a great deal of special care, particularly in the first few days and weeks and, critically, they needed a milk supplement to replace their mother's milk.

As all these factors came to light I realised that all the hard work, sleepless nights, treatment of endless bumps and bruises along with countless buckets of milk, had probably saved the lives of Rundi and Muku. The daily attention to every detail was absolutely critical in keeping them free from infection and calm enough to be handled and cared for. It hadn't been an easy undertaking as again and again I had to stand firm against the criticisms from many armchair experts who told me that elephants were wild animals and would survive far better without human intervention. Regardless of the rights and wrongs of culling elephant herds and rescuing young calves, to save them once and then abandon them in the wilderness made no sense at all. Two healthy, thriving baby elephants at the Mukuvisi Woodlands were proof enough of what had been the right way to proceed after the animals had been saved from culling operations.

The conflicts I had about the rights and wrongs of hand rearing baby elephants were always in the back of my mind and came to the fore again when I had a visit from a man who worked in a safari park in Canada. He had some very strong opinions about raising elephants.

"How do you discipline them?" Brian asked.

"Well at this stage it's mostly by the use of food and voice," I replied.

"That's alright now when they're still small and frightened, but what's going to happen when they are three metres tall and weigh a couple of tonnes?"

I didn't have an answer to Brian's question. I knew that Rundi and Muku would only be at the Mukuvisi Woodlands for a couple of years before being moved to a bigger game park. At this stage my mandate was to keep them alive, calm them down and get them used to being in contact with people. My predecessor at the Mukuvisi Woodlands hadn't kept any records on rearing and caring for orphaned baby elephants; there were no files to consult, no guidelines, no do's and don'ts, not even the recommended ingredients and proportions of the life saving milk and porridge formula. I was on a steep learning curve taking one day at a time. Aside from keeping them alive from one day to the next it was never far from my mind that however we treated and cared for Rundi and Muku now, when they were babies, would probably determine how they would behave with people for the rest of their lives.

"Let me show you how we discipline them in Canada," Brian said.

We were down at the platform with the elephants and my eyebrows went up when Brian said:

"When they are really young like this, elephant mothers discipline their calves by biting their tails."

I said nothing but swallowed rapidly to suffocate the little bubble of hysteria tickling my throat. I could just see me, Oscar or Simon bending down to bite Rundi's tail.

"Watch," Brian said. He put his hand at the base of Rundi's tail, just above the bristly brush, and pressed his finger nails into her, pinching her skin. The reaction was immediate. Rundi's ears went straight out, she bellowed, defecated and ran away.

"You see!" Brian said smiling. "That's how we discipline our elephants in Canada."

I smiled and nodded but still couldn't erase the image of an enormous elephant cow taking her calf's tail in her mouth and biting it!

I filed the information in my memory bank and once or twice in the months that followed gave Rundi's tail a strong pinch when things were getting out of control and it always produced the same reaction. Tail biting wasn't something I was happy with at all. Whenever I had the chance to watch elephants in the wild after that I always watched to see if an elephant cow did bite her calf's tail and can't say I ever did; perhaps wild elephants in Canada did!

One method of disciplining that I did see in elephant herds in the wild was the mother slapping the calf sharply on its back or buttocks with her trunk. Elephants in the wild were always interacting with each other and were very tactile: always smelling and touching but the trunk slap on the backside was a very different touch. When things with Rundi and Muku got out hand I found that swat on the backside was enough and infinitely preferable to tail biting, particularly because I wanted to rear Rundi and Muku as close to naturally as possible. There was, however, a fine line between a smack and a beating, just as there was between discipline and abuse.

Something else I learnt from Brian was put into practice immediately.

"Don't you give them toys?" he had asked as we stood on the platform looking down on Rundi and Muku.

"Toys?" I echoed.

"We give our elephants balls and batons and old tyres," Brian said, "it gives them something to do."

An enclosure of a few acres in a Canadian safari park could hardly be compared to 109 hectares of bush in a Zimbabwean game park filled with trees, dams and indigenous vegetation but I didn't dismiss the idea of toys. We had used small tree branches to help Rundi strengthen her trunk muscles when the elephants were in the boma and both she and Muku had spent hours playing with the wood.

The day after Brian's visit I introduced the elephants to toys to keep them occupied when they were hanging around at the platform. I point blank refused to contemplate balls or anything else plastic and instead gave them natural toys, much to the amusement of the workers. When I asked Oscar to bring a saw and told him what it was for, he shouted his great booming laugh, attracting the inquisitive attention of Ray and Simon who followed at a distance.

As always Rundi and Muku were hanging around at the platform. They had had their morning walk and buckets of milk and porridge and stood idly lifting puffs of dust onto their heads. As the procession made its way through the gate, they both immediately lumbered over to see what was going on.

"Those branches there Oscar," I said, pointing to the branches of a gum tree that were hanging over the fence line. By then Simon and Ray had arrived and using his much practised talent of delegating, Oscar handed the saw to Simon and told him to climb the tree and cut off the branches. The elephants had abandoned their dust bathing and came over to where we all stood beneath the giant gum trees. They loved to be a part of everything that was going on, being part of a herd was something that was undoubtedly a naturally instinctive part of their behaviour and we had become their herd. Rundi went around, smelling and touching all of us while Muku made a bee line for the saw and made a few valiant attempts at getting it away from Simon.

"Are you ready Simon?" I asked, eager to get this exercise underway before it descended into chaos. Simon nodded and climbed up into the tree.

"Let's try and get the elephants away from here; can you help me Ray?"

The last thing I wanted was a branch falling on an elephants head. Ray and I watched from a distance with the elephants. What a picture it would have made: Ray stroking Rundi while she sucked my hand, Muku sucking Rundi's ear, Simon up a tree and Oscar smoking one of his foul smelling newspaper cigarettes while directing operations.

The four large eucalyptus branches, leaves and all were dragged away from the fence and dumped in the grass and near the platform. Rundi and Muku immediately set to destroying their new toys. They stripped leaves, snapped twigs and peeled bark. We left them to it and I was delighted to see them still at it later that day and for many days afterwards. Muku seemed particularly preoccupied with the toys and would often walk around either holding a stick or balancing it on top of his head. Here was an elephant with an obvious sense of humour.

Elephant toys became a very important part of rearing and caring for Rundi and Muku because not only did they provide a release from boredom, they also created a welcome diversion when something unpleasant had to be done. As the elephants grew, so did their need for toys and the game committee members and I were always on the lookout for natural things for them to play with. We would all go on game patrols with empty bags and return with items we picked up on our walks. Beth was particularly conscientious when it came to looking for toys for the elephants. When she and her teenage son Peter went out on game patrols the elephants always went with them. If you happened to be at the viewing platform when Beth and Peter returned it was a delight to watch. Rundi first, then Beth with a bag in each hand, followed by Peter with a rucksack on his back and a bag or two in his hands and at the rear was Muku. Arriving at the platform the toys would be removed and spread out for the elephants. Rundi and Muku would eagerly smell, touch and pick up each treasure accompanied by much head shaking and nodding, ear slapping and intent sniffing.

Because I insisted that the toys could only be natural things, the elephants usually proceeded to eat their toys so we had to become more and more inventive in our offerings. Branches of eucalyptus were always good as the scented leaves weren't appetizing. You never knew what would keep the elephants occupied; sometimes it would be a piece of lichen, a lump of moss, the flowering tops of bull rushes or even a bird's nest. Other favourites were strips of bark, lengths of vine or creeper, hard lumps of anthill soil and a particular favourite was ostrich feathers. Muku especially loved the feathers. He would hold a feather in the tip of his trunk and then curling his trunk on to the top of his head with the feather sailing like a flag, he would wander off. Sometimes Muku would walk far out into the bush with his feather flag flying.

SIX

....

"Falcons! That's a fantastic suggestion!" a committee member said. "What a wonderful idea," someone else chipped in.

"What do you think Cathy?" the Chairman asked but I didn't have a chance to respond.

The suggestion had come up during another long winded, committee meeting and been so enthusiastically taken up that before I knew it the idea had been proposed, seconded and agreed upon. A falconry display was to be held at the Mukuvisi Woodlands and the falconers would fly their birds inside the game park.

My head was immediately whirling with tasks: tickets, small change, parking, the kiosk, security, toilets, the platform and, of course, the elephants. As the word elephants settled in my head, my mind went back a couple of sentences: the falconers would fly their birds inside the game park, where the elephants were! Oh no, this was an inevitable incident waiting to happen; let's hope it would only be an incident not an accident!

As the big day approached the jobs were delegated; Oscar, Simon, Ray and Joçam had their work cut out for them. The platform, a permanent dust trap, had to be spotless: cupboards, walls, floors and, chairs. Grass along paths and buildings needed a trim and ponds in the tortoise and crocodile enclosures needed topping up and vegetation trimming.

My job was the office, organising and admin; Ray's was the kiosk and toilets; and Oscar's was supervising Joçam and Simon, dispatching them wherever they were needed. As I explained everything and ran through the tasks to be done, Oscar got the strange glazed look in his eyes that I had seen so many times before; Ray fiddled nervously and Simon played with a box of matches in his pocket. Everyone was tense and enough had been said so we all got to work.

This wasn't our first big event but everything had to be perfect. It was hard to know in advance how many people to expect but it would be probably be a hundred or more. I knew only too well that if one thing was wrong it could so easily damage our reputation which was the last thing we wanted in our continual struggle to attract members and donations.

The day before the falconry display we were all exhausted. Oscar half-heartedly cleaned the office while Simon mumbled and muttered in the car park as he bent down picking up cigarette butts, mostly his. Ray and I were buried in mountains of food in the kiosk and exhaustedly put potato crisps onto shelves, tipped coffee into jars, chocolates into bowls and packed drinks into the fridge. At last, when it was too dark to see and after about ten cups of coffee, I called everyone together for the final meeting and pep talk.

"Thanks everyone! You've all worked so hard and everything is looking fantastic. We've done well!"

I turned to Simon to talk about the one thing that was worrying me the most; it had been giving me sleepless nights and was something over which I had absolutely no control at all.

"Elephants Simon! Tomorrow you've got to keep those elephants under control when the falconers arrive to fly their birds."

Simon smiled wearily and by the bemused look on his face I suddenly wondered if he understood what this whole falconry thing was and what was going to happen.

"Do you understand what's going to happen tomorrow Simon?"

"Oh yes! Some people are bringing birds for people to see."

"Not only to see Simon. To watch them fly."

Simon's face creased into a confused frown.

"Some senior school boys and others are bringing falcons and letting them fly in the game park," I explained.

"Falkels?"

"Falcons! Hawks! Birds of prey." Simon still looked confused so I pulled the bird book off the shelf and showed him a picture of a black Sparrowhawk, a big bird of prey that we often saw in the Mukuvisi Woodlands.

"Oh," he grinned, "falkels!"

"They are bringing birds like this to do a falconry show. The birds have been trained to hunt and come back to a person." I didn't know how much he understood but we all saw the Sparrowhawks often because they nested every year in the big gum trees along the boundary fence. Simon grinned happily and nodded his head.

"You'll see tomorrow Simon, but you've got to keep Rundi and Muku out of the way."

"OK, OK," he nodded reassuringly. That was familiar ground.

"Have lots of vegetables ready, fruit, horse cubes, sticks and branches to keep them occupied." Simon nodded as I reeled off the list, this was common ground for him, he knew what was needed. "And you stay with them all the time Simon. Don't leave them alone for a minute when we've got the guys flying their birds in the game park."

Finally we all stumbled home and even though I knew that everything was ready, I dreaded the next day. Oscar would spend the whole day in the office, taking money, giving directions, answering questions and doing what he did best, chatting and public relations. Raymond would spend the day in the kiosk, pouring cold drinks, tea and coffee and serving food. This was exactly what Ray did best and always with a great sense of humour and wonderful smile. Simon, poor Simon, would be solely in charge of the elephants. It was what he did best and he was the best man, the only man, for that job. I would be meeting and greeting, checking on and relieving the workers, directing the falconers and resolving any problems that cropped up. I didn't get much sleep that night, mentally going through endless lists in my head. By five the next morning I was up and by six thirty was at work. A quick chat and then we were all busy, putting the finishing touches on weeks of preparation.

I walked around. The toilets were shining, loo rolls plentiful, soap in the hand basins, no dripping taps for a change. Tortoises had piles of tomatoes and lettuce, the water in the pond was lapping the edges and the terrapins were basking on logs in the early morning sun. The crocs, mean and ugly as ever, lay slumbering on the sand bank we had made for them; all the missiles that were regularly thrown at them had been removed: drink bottles, stones, sticks, plastic bags, pens and pencils. Down at the platform Simon and Joçam were busy. The elephants were milling around, helping unload hay from wheelbarrows, manure from shovels and hats from heads! On the viewing platform itself where all the spectators would stand to watch the show, everything looked fantastic. Chairs were stacked out of the way; the skulls, bones and snakes in bottles had been dusted down and the view from the platform was as serene as ever: the wide open vlei, trees in the background, dam in the foreground and elephants below. In the kiosk Ray was busy: the urn was filled and switched on, there was plenty of milk and the drinks in the fridge were icy cold.

As the first car drove in I took a deep breath. Falkel day had arrived!

Oscar and Ray had their work cut out for them almost immediately. Leaving them to it I went to supervise the elephants' breakfast. I had decided that Rundi and Muku should have their milk and porridge earlier than normal, an attempt to get them really calm before the mornings activities which were due to start at ten. Simon had already taken them on their usual morning walk and as they slurped their milk and porridge, he assured me that they were very tired and would go to sleep at any minute. Milk finished, the elephants picked uninterestedly through the pile of vegetables we had put out, obviously not hungry. By now quite a few people were up on the platform and there was a buzz of voices in the background. Rundi rubbed her eye with the tip of her trunk and I breathed a great sigh of relief when she ambled off into the shade under the platform, followed almost immediately by Muku. I called Simon and we left together.

"Just stay outside now Simon and do not wake them."

"Aaah no, I don't wake them," he replied.

Knowing there were already people waiting for action photographs, I had my doubts and raised my eyebrows. Simon looked sheepish; enough said; I had recently caught him accepting a ten dollar note in exchange for calling the elephants back from a walk so that tourists could take photos of them.

Over the next hour a steady stream of guests arrived and the car park filled up. I took the opportunity to learn as much as I could. I had no idea how involved falconry was. Teaching school boys to be falconers wasn't a club or hobby that lasted a term or two, it was a commitment that continued throughout senior school and beyond. For the first two years the boys would be apprentices: cleaning pens, weighing birds, keeping records and learning about the anatomy and physiology of falcons. Each boy had his own bird and would take care of all of its needs: cleaning, feeding, handling, weighing and later flying for prey. The apprentice falconer had to attend to his bird every day, gaining a rapport with the bird and establishing a routine of handling and feeding times.

School boys learnt to be falconers with African Goshawks or Ovambo Sparrowhawks. It was drilled into the boys from the first day: "Bring hawk food!" and this couldn't be a lump of mince meat or chunk of steak it had to be prey, not gutted or de-feathered: hawks needed feathers and bone for their digestive systems to function.

Every day the boy would handle his bird: train it to step onto a perch and a gloved hand. The bird was weighed every day; every gram of food was critical and the amount of food adjusted accordingly to get the bird to its optimum weight. The hawk had to be kept in peak condition: lean enough so that it would fly and return to the handler for food but not too heavy so that it wouldn't return to the falconer. Apprentice falconers learnt about castings, the regurgitated feathers and bone that the bird expelled within 12 hours of feeding, and how critical it was to check that the castings had been be expelled if the bird was to fly and return to the falconer.

Each falcon had its own travelling crate, a wooden box with air holes; dark and secure, excluding light, preventing the bird from getting startled or alarmed. The bird wears a leather hood, its beak and neck exposed but eyes covered to exclude light. When the falcon has its hood on it is effectively blindfolded and immediately sits still and is at ease, allowing it to be handled and moved. Falcons have extremely good eyesight and can see a newspaper from a kilometre away, critical for spotting prey and for seeing the falconer. On its legs the bird wears leather anklets to which jesses or thin leather strips are attached and these are what the falconer holds on to when the falcon sits on his gloved fist. A pair of small bells is attached to the hawk's legs and these enable the falconer to trace the bird when it's flying free. Always assuming the bells were cruel I realised how wrong I was when the falconer explained to me that the bells actually forewarned the prey, giving it a chance to get away from the falcon.

There was just one more thing to understand, the actual flying of the falcon but I glanced at my watch and could see I had run out of time; the rest I would have to learn by watching the display.

Reg Querl was the falconry instructor who had come with the boys from Peterhouse School and I ran through the plans with him: where the boys would go, how I would let them in and out of the game gate and Simon would take them onto the wall of the pan which was where they would fly their birds from. The wall of the pan was less than a hundred meters from the game gate giving the guests on the game viewing platform above an excellent view of the display. It was nearly winter and the grass was shimmering and golden in the mid morning sunlight. Dense stands of Natal red top grass (*Rhynchelytrum*) dipped and swayed in the gentle breeze looking like a river of pink and white running through the grassland.

Leaving Peter Brookes Ball to introduce the falconers I moved to the far side of the platform, ready to escort the first group of boys. Reg Querl gave a short talk on falcons and falconry and the audience were spellbound when he took out his bird and it sat on his gloved fist, regal and upright, the hood adding to the mystery and intrigue. Reg had a Peregrine Falcon while the boys had African Goshawks and an Ovambo Sparrowhawk.

I escorted the first group of boys down from the platform to the game gate and Simon walked them out onto the wall of the pan. With Reg up on the platform explaining the proceedings, the first teenager got ready. At his waist he had a leather bag, on his hand a long, padded leather glove. The boy removed his bird's hood, dropping it into the bag while holding the leather strips hanging from the bird's feet. Swinging his arm back, the boy cast the African Goshawk up into the air and it took flight, making for a termite mound some distance away in the vlei. People on the platform raised binoculars but even without them we could easily see the bird's distinctive white wings with black bars and two white spots on its dark tail. The Goshawk circled the group of trees on the termite mound a couple of times before it settled on one and then turned to look at the falconer. The youngster left the bird to rest for a couple of minutes before calling it back.

"Hoy! Hoy!" he called, holding his gloved hand up, a piece of feathered meat gripped in his fingers, visible to the bird. The Goshawk lifted up from the tree and returned, gliding down to land on the falconer's glove to eat the piece of meat the boy held for it. The crowd was delighted and applause broke out.

I breathed a sigh of relief, so far so good and no sign of elephants!

The young falconers took turns to fly their birds and everything was going so well that I began to relax and enjoy the display myself. When the first group of boys had finished the second group went in; they were obviously less experienced but did very well and the crowd on the platform clapped and whistled as they started back towards the game gate.

Waiting at the gate to let the boys out, I heard a swell of laughter growing in the audience and turned round to see Rundi and Muku bearing down on the retreating boys. I had already unlocked the gates to let another three young falconers in but I could see there was going to be an issue with the elephants.

"Just wait here guys, we're going to have to get the elephants out of the way first."

With the second group safely waiting outside the gate I gestured for the first group of boys to hurry; they didn't need much encouraging and managed to get out just in time. By then the elephants were running, straight at the game gate. I slammed the gate shut and snapped on the padlock. Rundi swung round in a circle to avoid hitting the gate, the cloud of dust she stirred up adding to the tension. Muku bellowed as I stood behind the locked gate, my pulse racing.

There was a lot of excited chatter from the people on the platform but I didn't dare turn round and look up at them.

"Everyone OK?"

The boys nodded; the group who were waiting to go into the game park looking far more anxious than those who had just come out with two elephants hot on their heels.

"Can you all just go and wait in the shade under that tree while we get the elephants calmed down?"

Leaving the boys chattering excitedly I went back to the game gate. Simon, a huge grin on his face, was coming towards me. At that moment I didn't know if his smile was one of amusement or embarrassment but it didn't matter, what mattered was to get the elephants calmed down and things under control as quickly as possible. Just two words were needed.

"Cubes Simon?"

He nodded, disappearing into a store- room under the platform, returning with a bucket containing a few handfuls of cubes. The moment the elephants saw the bucket they were putty in our hands, following Simon away from the gate, gently taking cubes out of his hand, all the excitement of boys and falcons, running and dust gone in an instant.

The people on the platform loved it; some were clapping, others laughing and as Simon walked slowly back towards the platform the elephants followed, dipping their trunks into the bucket, putting cubes into their mouths. Someone on the platform called down to Simon and he stopped to respond to their question. Out of the corner of his eye he saw me waving my arms, gesticulating to him to take the elephants right away, under the platform, into their stable and completely out of sight. This was the falconers' day; the youngsters had travelled all the way from Marondera and gone to a lot of trouble with their birds; this was their day to be in the spotlight, not the elephants'.

With Rundi and Muku out of sight and when they hadn't re-emerged after a little while, I escorted the next group of young falconers into the game park and up the grassy bank onto the wall of the pan. No sign of elephants, I smiled at the youngsters, nodded to Reg up on the platform and we got underway again. Everything went smoothly for a while until one of the youngest falconers couldn't get his bird to return. The Goshawk flew off and perched in a small Acacia tree from where it refused to move. Falconers train their birds to return to perch on their glove but also to a lure. This was a long piece of string attached to a wooden block. The falconer ties a piece of prey such as a strip of meat or a wing to the end of the string, holds the block and swings the lure in the air above his head to attract his bird. When the hawk comes in for the lure the falconer drops it to the ground and can then secure the bird while it feeds on the prey. Some hawks feel less pressured to return to a lure then to a gloved hand and this is what the young falconer used now. Again and again the youngster circled the lure over his head but the Goshawk sat dead still in the Acacia tree, studiously ignoring the young falconer.

After some time, red in the face and looking distinctly uncomfortable, the youngster began whistling repeatedly for the bird. The crowd on the platform were already tittering nervously but when the volume increased I groaned. The elephants were back. The whistling had obviously been too much of a temptation for them to ignore and out they came: jauntily, ears flapping, trunks swaying, eyes shining; you could almost see them laughing!

I glared, Simon shrugged but now it was pointless. The elephants were on a definite mission: a boy, a bird, high pitched whistling and a little fluffy grey thing being circled in the air on the end of a long string. This was clearly irresistible and there was nothing Simon or I could do to persuade the elephants otherwise. Rundi and Muku lumbered across to where the nervous, red-faced teenager stood desperately circling his lure and whistling to the unmoving falcon. I could see by the way Rundi held her trunk up, that this was not an aggressive move, just inquisitive. Muku trundled along behind her, slowly swinging his head from side to side, the tip of his trunk slightly curled up and repeatedly touching the dusty ground as he walked. From previous bad experience I knew that the worst thing any of us could do was run. By then I had unlocked the gate and was going across to the pan wall.

"Don't run!" I called out to the youngster. "It's OK, just don't run!"

My warning came too late. Unfortunately the closer the elephants got, the more frightened the schoolboy got. He'd had enough, his arm was tired from endlessly circling the lure, he was out of breath from whistling, it was hot and everyone was laughing. The boy took to his heels, closely followed by two elephants. Then the African Goshawk also took fright and flew off even further into the distance, circled a couple of times, finally coming to rest high up in a gum tree, well out of the way of the elephants and the unfolding drama. Looking near to tears the boy stopped at the Acacia tree where his falcon had been and finally stood still. I got to him at the same time as Rundi; the youngster was shaking and out of breath.

"Don't worry," I said, stroking Rundi, putting myself between the elephant and the youngster. "She won't hurt you. She just wants to smell you."

The schoolboy grinned nervously at me as Rundi sniffed his face with her sticky, wet nose and Muku made repeated attempts to eat the falconers lure. The crowd on the platform was nearly hysterical by now and when I led the youngster out of the game gate, they rose as one and gave him a standing ovation, whistling, cheering and clapping. His red face deepened in colour but no one noticed because the attention turned back to the elephants who had managed to steal the show yet again. Simon scattered tomatoes, orange halves and cubes all over the ground below the platform and they settled down to eat quite contentedly.

After a while we let another group of falconers in, the elephants ignored them and the programme got back on track. The teenager's falcon stayed on its perch in the gum tree and much later when the Falconry display was over and everyone had gone for lunch, I went back into the game park with the youngster and he managed to attract the bird to the lure and retrieve it. It was hard to know why the bird hadn't responded to the calls of the falconer earlier. It was possible that it was slightly overweight and not hungry but it could just as easily have seen something that caught its eye and frightened it, such as our resident Wahlberg's eagles. In that case the falcon's natural instinct would have been to keep completely still and not respond to calls, whistles or circling lures until the threat had passed.

With the falconry display over things slowly got back to normal; a hundred and ninety eight people had attended the event and it took a while to clean up the mess and get back to our usual routines. It wasn't long before I turned my attention to the next big task and it was one I wouldn't be able to do without the presence of the elephants. Every year as winter approached we would start work on the boundaries of the game park to protect the area from fire.

The task consisted of clearing two strips of vegetation, each a metre wide, with three metres in between them. When that had been done we would burn the grass between the two strips and be left with a five metre wide fire break. This five metre fire break helped to stop fires spreading into the game area but also provided a safe place to back burn from. Without tractors or machinery of any sort, creating the fire breaks was an entirely manual operation and was a big task. I took on six casual workers who, together with three of the permanent employees started the job of clearing the strips. Armed with hoes and rakes, the nine men went into the game park and got started. I set them a daily quota and they could go home once they'd completed their allocation. This was a great incentive and everyone got to work at a great pace. Rundi and Muku were out on their morning walk so there were nothing to slow down the fire break clearing and I left to the sound of men laughing as they worked and dust hanging in the air.

A couple of hours later I went back to the platform and watched

Rundi and Muku finish their milk and porridge before going off to lie in their dusty beds. After checking on the progress of the fire break clearing, I went back to the office but not for long because about forty minutes later Raymond came running into the office.

"Come quickly. There's been an accident with the elephants."

This was my worst nightmare.

As I locked the office Ray told me what he knew. He had been cleaning up around the tortoise enclosures when he heard shouting from somewhere down by the platform. Locking the kiosk Ray got half way to the platform when the shouting grew louder and this time he could hear the word 'Nzou' (Shona for elephant). As Ray got closer to the platform he could see people on the main road pointing to the game fence. He looked over the platform railing, saw the elephants weren't there and decided to come and call me. Whether there had actually been an accident or not I didn't know but I dropped everything, grabbed a key for the game area and Ray and I ran towards the platform.

We were both out of breath when we got to the game gate, it was a fair distance from the office to the platform and ever since the elephants had arrived I'd learned how fast I could run! As we got to the gate I looked across to the dusty hollows where I'd last seen Rundi and Muku sleeping but they weren't there. Ray and I went into the game area and ran along the newly cleared firebreak to the corner where I'd left the men working earlier. As we turned the corner we immediately saw the problem. One of the casual workers was perched half way up a tree and another had climbed the game fence and was clinging onto the diamond mesh. Below them Rundi was calmly having a dust bath in the soft soil on the newly cleared firebreak. Curling her trunk she scooped up little 'handfuls' of soil and puffed them over her head and seemed totally uninterested in either the man hanging on the fence or the one sitting up a tree.

"Muku's the problem, look Ray!"

Muku had picked up a hoe abandoned by one of the workers and was holding it with his trunk, casually swinging it from side to side, the sun glinting on the sharp, shiny edge of the tool. There was no sign of any of the others who were supposed to be working on the fire break and it took a while to get to the bottom of what was had happened. It turned out that the three Mukuvisi workers had gone off for tea, leaving the six casuals, who wanted to finish their day's quota, working in the game area.

Not long after the others had gone for tea, the elephants had arrived. Muku had made a beeline for a hoe that had been left lying on the ground, picked it up and began swinging it around. The casual workers panicked; four ran into the bush, one climbed a tree and the other was trying to get over the game fence but had got to what he thought was a safe height and then just hung on for dear life.

"Come down, it's OK," I called to the man up the tree.

"What about the elephants?"

"Don't worry, they're fine! It's safe, you can come down."

"Look," Ray called to the men as he patted and stroked Rundi, "there's no problem with them."

It took a bit more talking and persuading to get the men to come down and even more coaxing to get them to come and stand next to me so I could introduce them to the elephants. Calling Rundi and Muku over and gently retrieving the stolen hoe from Muku, I could almost feel the men shaking next to me but they managed to stand still while the elephants sniffed them from head to toe, dabbing little wet trunk tips on heads and necks, faces and feet.

"We thought the elephant was going to attack us with the hoe!" one of them said and we all laughed, the tension melting away as we stood there in the golden grass next to the two elephants. These casual workers would certainly have a good story to tell their kids when they got home tonight.

There was still no sign of the other men who had run off into the bush but no doubt they would reappear once the elephants had gone. I left Ray with the two casual workers and asked him to stay there until the others had come back from tea to avoid any more incidents. Heading back to the platform I called Rundi and Muku and they followed me without hesitation and were soon happily back in their dusty hollows having their mid morning sleep in the sun. From then on tea time was staggered so that the casuals were never alone in the game park again. As funny as the incident had been, it could so easily have turned into something else. Most people had never seen an elephant close up before and for many the only knowledge of these grey giants of the bush was when they came to raid crops and snack on vegetable plots at night. To have an encounter with two elephants so close that you could hear their vocal rumbles, see their long black eyelashes and the wrinkles on their skin must have been terrifying. Add Muku waving a hoe around like a drum majorette and the whole encounter had understandably been just too much to bear.

After their initial encounter with the elephants the casual workers got on happily with their job, proudly bragging about their close shave with an elephant swinging a hoe. Once the elephants realised that something was going on inside the game area, they never left the workers alone. They seemed to delight in tagging along behind the casuals, rescuing tasty morsel that were unearthed, having endless dust baths in newly cleared soft sand and generally getting in the way. Muku had a passion for discarded hoes, snatching the implements whenever they were put down and then refusing to give them back. Rundi however found that the casuals came with their own lunch which they carried in pots which were tied up in plastic bags. More than once I was asked to replace a lunch that Rundi had destroyed by grabbing the bag and running away with it, the pot rattling crazily, before inevitably ending up with the food spilt all over the ground.

Rundi and Muku spent their days following their casual workers clearing the fire break and if ever we couldn't find them, that's where they were. Muku had a nasty experience one morning when the men were clearing the fire break under some flowering gum trees which were full of bees. Muku picked up a piece of grass which must have had a bee clinging to it and he was stung on the tip of his trunk. Muku went wild, bellowing and roaring and with ears and tail out he swung round in circles, defecating everywhere before running away trumpeting. Rundi, unbitten but obviously frightened by Muku's behaviour, put her ears out and raced after him. Sometime later when Muku had calmed down and come home, all there was to see was a small swelling on the tip of his trunk; an ailment soon forgotten with a bucket of milk!

The highlight of the elephants' day was always milk and porridge. Rundi and Muku each had their own bucket of milk and even with it being three quarters full it took less than five minutes for it to be drained. The grey trunks were dipped about five centimetres below the surface of the liquid and then followed noisy slurping of the thick mixture. A trunk full was sucked up, the trunk lifted out of the bucket, curled round and squirted into the elephant's mouth. It didn't take long before the buckets were empty but strangely Rundi always left a little bit of milk at the bottom of the bucket. I wasn't sure if she didn't like the feel of the bucket against her trunk, didn't have a strong enough suck to reach the dregs or if she left some deliberately to protect herself from the boisterous and greedy Muku. As soon as he had finished his milk, and he always finished first, Muku would stretch his nose over and drop it into Rundi's bucket. Then, with sticky wet noses, ringed with tide marks of milk, the two elephants would sniff around each other's mouths. I didn't know why they did that, perhaps they were checking they'd both had the same thing? When Rundi and Muku were satisfied that the buckets really were empty and there wasn't going to be any more, they would retreat to a spot in the sun, lie down and go to sleep.

Sometimes they went into their stable under the platform but more often as they grew older, they lay out in the sun in the well moulded dusty hollows they'd made for themselves.

Baby elephants sleep lying on their sides, legs straight out with their trunk tucked protectively over their mouth. It was such a novelty to see elephants lying prone like this and something you very rarely saw in the wild. People used to believe that elephants couldn't lie down because of their enormous size which it was assumed put enormous pressure on their internal organs. Zoo keepers disproved the belief showing adult elephants do lie down but usually only for an hour or two at time. They also rested by leaning their heads on trees and, something we had often seen with Coke, they would often rest their trunks against low branches of trees.

When they slept in the sun Rundi and Muku lay so still that they looked dead. Their breathing slowed down and because their stomachs were full of milk it made it difficult to see the rise and fall of their breathing. I was often called out by tourists who anxiously rushed into my office to tell me the elephants were dead. It was always frustrating to be called away from my desk and the mountains of paperwork by a tourist saying:

"Come quickly, the elephants are dead."

I did try telling people they weren't dead, only sleeping, but it always sounded callous and uncaring so nine times out of ten I'd leave the stack of papers, trudge down to the platform and show a tourist the small but inevitable sign of life. At each exhalation, the tip of the trunk lying in the soft sand would cause a small puff of dust. This was proof of life, not easy to notice if you didn't know where to look. As frustrating as the interruptions to paperwork were, my spirits always lifted when I stood at the platform looking down on Rundi and Muku. What loving creatures they were and how privileged I was to be a part of this time of their lives.

SEVEN

....

eturning from a game patrol one day I asked Simon to come with
some horse cubes. It was later in the morning, the elephants had
had their buckets of milk and porridge, Simon had returned from his tea
break and everything felt calm and sleepy. The sun was warm, flowering
grass swayed in a gentle breeze and a couple of zebra were drinking at
the pan in front of the platform. Conditions were quiet and balmy; ideal
for what I hoped would be a brief and easy intervention into Rundi's
latest veterinary problem.

"I want to do something about Rundi's ear," I said to Simon. He
raised his eyes and smiled nervously but I put my fingers to my lips,
wanting to keep the whole thing as low key and unobtrusive as ever.
Muku had sucked a hole right through Rundi's ear and it was time to do
something about it.

"I'll go for the medicine while you get the cubes but let's be very
quiet about this so they don't suspect anything's going on."

I must have been gone for about ten minutes and groaned when I
got back to find three tourists at the game viewing platform waiting to
watch the show. Simon loved being photographed with the elephants
and there was no way the tourists were going to leave if there was a
chance of seeing some action. I hated treating the elephants in front
of spectators but since Simon had already scattered cubes everywhere

I knew it would be almost impossible to lure them away from there and walk them all the way to the boma. Walking the elephants to the boma to treat them was always a last resort but something we did if we needed to get them into a confined space. I knew that walking them to the boma now, while there were cubes scattered all over the ground at the platform, wouldn't be easy and so I decided to carry on where we were.

Muku's persistent sucking on Rundi's ear, almost always the same ear, had caused the skin to be soft, puffy and wet; it looked a bit like pruney fingers that you get from having your hands in water for too long! Rundi's ear now had a wet, open wound which, when not being sucked, was always covered in flies and you could see daylight through the hole. I explained to Simon that I wanted to wash the wound on Rundi's ear and dab it with iodine. While I did this Simon's task was to divert Muku with sticks, feathers and horse cubes.

I made a small pile of food on the ground for Rundi and while she ate I cleaned her ear with wet, antiseptic saturated cotton wool. At first Rundi took no notice at all but then I had to rub quite hard as the skin was sticky with saliva and a crust of mud. Rudi got a bit agitated and rumbled loudly when I rubbed too hard and tried to chip off the mud but the food pile was a good diversion and I was able to carry on. Taking a clean pad of cotton wool I soaked it in iodine and pressed it firmly into the wound. Rundi didn't like that; she rumbled in a deep tone and reversed a few steps away from me. I waited a minute and moved in again, this time trying to get some iodine onto the underside of her ear as well.

That did it! As soon as I lifted her ear Rundi bellowed and crashed her head into me. She had obviously had enough of my ministrations. As I caught my breath and rubbed my hip where her head had made contact I noticed that Muku was looking at us. His eyes widened, never a good sign, and to my intense irritation and the enormous amusement of the tourists, he walked over and immediately started sucking Rundi's newly treated ear. I pushed him off and everyone laughed, including me, at ate sight of this big soppy elephants huge iodine stained tongue.

"Aaah, it is hopeless," Simon said stating the obvious, pointing to Muku's red tongue. I couldn't have put it better.

"Can we get a close up of that?" one of the tourists called down from the platform and I left to the sound of clicking cameras and much laughter. I would have to think of another plan.

I treated Rundi's ear with iodine for another four days but as Muku's tongue got redder and redder I knew I was wasting my time. By then the pin prick of daylight through Rundi's ear had enlarged and was now a clearly visible hole and always clustered with flies. I was getting worried about infection and maggots, although Muku's sucking would probably lessen the chance of the latter. The ears of elephants play such a critical role in the whole cooling system of an elephant and in an adult bull they are over a metre wide and almost two metres high; as tall as most people! Elephants don't have sweat glands in their skin but the underside of their ear is covered with a network of blood vessels very close to the surface; the continual flapping of their ears acts like a radiator, helping to cool their blood, apparently by as much as 4 degrees Celsius. Apparently the vein patterns on the underside of an elephant's ears are different in every individual and researchers use this to identify individuals in the wild. I knew that holes and tears in elephants' ears were very common, caused by getting snagged on sticks and branches or damaged in other ways in the bush and that researchers used the cuts, holes and jagged edges as ways of identifying individual elephants. I wondered if Rundi would later be identified by the vein patterns on her ears or would it be the holes left from Muku's sucking!

When I phoned Morna for advice on how to treat the puffy, fly encrusted wound on Rundi's ear, she thought for a minute and then said:

"I think you need something on there that dries really fast. Why not try gentian violet?"

I switched from iodine to gentian violet and the stain on my fingers and Muku's tongue changed from red to purple. Every day I dabbed and Muku sucked. His tongue looked obscene, as did my hands and nails but Rundi's ear was getting worse. All around the wound it was red and puffy and often had congealed blood and a cluster of flies feeding on the edge of it. Again I changed my medication, this time from gentian violet to an antibiotic aerosol spray. By now what should have been a quick and simple procedure had become a major daily drama. As soon as Rundi saw me coming in the gate wearing my grey dust coat and carrying a bag or bottle, she would spread her ears, shake her head and move away. I couldn't treat her on my own as she wouldn't let me get anywhere near her so Oscar, Simon and Ray had been recruited to distract Muku and try and hold Rundi.

A bad situation soon got totally out of control. It was school holidays and there were two young boys, aged about nine and ten, who followed me around, always in search of a new adventure. Justin and Gary would start to giggle as soon as they saw me reach for my dustcoat.

"Going to do Rundi's ear?" one of them would ask with a note of high pitched hysteria already in his voice.

The other boy would titter nervously.

"Go on, push off you two," I'd reply but my words didn't make them leave, instead it started them off and they would race off laughing crazily, clutching their stomachs with spontaneous, uncontrollable mirth.

Arriving at the gate with Oscar, Ray and Simon, we went in quietly. I could hear suppressed giggles coming from the game viewing platform above us. Looking up I caught a glimpse of Justin and Gary who ducked down as soon as they saw me; their giggling increasing.

Muku was not in sight and although I knew he must be nearby I got started immediately. Oscar and Ray stood on one side of Rundi's head and Simon stood in front with a pocketful of horse cubes while I immediately started to clean and spray the wound.

"Look out, Muku's coming," a voice from above called out and both boys burst into helpless laugher as Muku barged in on the proceedings, knocked my hand in mid spray and attached his great purple tongue to Rundi's newly treated ear.

With the workers muttering and me grumbling we gave up and left. As soon as we had closed the gate out of the game area, Justin and Gary came scampering towards us from the platform, giggling and spluttering, tears of laughter streaming down their faces. I had learnt that is was best to completely ignore them when they got like this because if I said anything at all, even just 'go-away' they would double up in hysterics and collapse on the ground.

The next day I changed my tactics.

"Aren't you going to do Rundi's ear?" one of the boys asked.

"Not today," I replied and both boys looked at me with disappointment on their faces. I had decided that I needed to break the routine of treating the ear at the same time of day; Rundi had got used to my timing and was always in a nervous state when I went down to the platform. I went about my day as normal, got Justin and Gary to help with other little jobs around the place, which they loved, and at about three in the afternoon they gave up waiting for elephant ear time and went home.

Leaving my grey dust coat in the little prefabricated office, I put a small plastic bag in my trouser pocket and went into the game park, innocently calling to Rundi and Muku to come for a walk with me. I had broken the routine and the elephants came happily swaying over to me, heads shaking, trunks touching me and lots of rumbly greetings. I set out purposefully towards the trees on the far side of the wetland. When we reached what I knew was a favourite feeding place, I waited a few minutes until the elephants were stuffing their mouths and then I opened the little plastic bag in my pocket. I took out a thick pad of cotton wool I had prepared beforehand and it was dripping in Friars Balsam. This was my new remedy, a favourite cure for all sorts of ailments used by my mother in law, and neither of the elephants took any notice at all as I casually drenched the sore on Rundi's ear, back and front, with Friars Balsam. After a while I called them to follow me but both of the elephants ignored me and carried on feeding so I left them there and headed back on my own.

The next morning I was delighted to see there was a hard crusty scab on Rundi's ear and it didn't look as if Muku had been sucking on it at all. That afternoon I repeated my secret mission and within a week the wound had healed up completely. The raw, inflamed, blistering skin was back to normal and the only tell tale sign of previous trouble was the small hole that permanently marked her ear. For some time Muku stopped sucking that ear completely, either because it was painful and Rundi pushed him off or because of the foul tasting Friars Balsam. He sucked her other ear every now and again but apparently not with as much relish and later went back to sucking her pierced ear but never as frequently as before; perhaps he was beginning to grow up and become more secure in himself and his surroundings.

By autumn 1987 the effects of the drought were beginning to be felt in many ways in the game park. As winter approached the vegetation lost its lush lustre. Deciduous trees had their last dusty leaves pulled off by the cooling wind and the grass got browner and drier as the sap receded into the roots. The water level in the two small dams got lower and lower, exposing vegetation that had been submerged since December. As the water levels dropped the animals had to walk further into the water to find a clean spot to drink from, the edges always churned up and water clouded with mud. Many of the animals, particularly the zebra and wildebeest, walked in single file when going to water and little trails through the grass turned into paths and then sunken, narrow, well worn gullies. Each season had its own problems and the beginning of winter was no exception. From my regular collection of dung samples, Roaland Jooste at the government Veterinary Department reported the presence of liver fluke and asked me to collect samples of the fluke's intermediate host so they could establish the degree of infestation. Snail collecting moved to the top of the agenda.

Dressed in my oldest clothes, green gumboots, grey dustcoat and carrying plastic bags filled with wet cotton wool I set out one afternoon to collect snails. This was a day when I didn't really want company but Rundi and Muku could not be persuaded to stay at home. Seeking the easiest route I pushed through the tall dry scratchy grass to the edge of the small Chiraura River. There was no flowing water left and the river consisted of a series of narrow, slimy, stagnant pools covered with water striders (*Gerridae*). Very half heartedly I ran my fingers through the mud at the edge of a couple of pools: nothing at all, not a snail to be found. I wasn't enthusiastic about the task and even less so as Rundi and Muku fiddled around in the filthy water either blowing bubbles in the slime or squirting themselves with the runny sludge. Splashed, smelly and annoyed, I decided the job would be much easier at one of the two dams. Changing direction I clambered though the dense clumps of grass along the now dry spillway to get to the pan in front of the platform. Then on the wind I could hear voices and looking up saw I was being watched by a group of tourists. There were many jobs I had to do in front of an audience but collecting snails wasn't one of them. I beat a hasty retreat, followed of course by my shadows, the elephants.

The second dam was shielded by towering grass and dense, spreading clumps of reeds and rushes. I waded cautiously through the shallows, aiming for some floating water lilies. The elephants followed. I tried to turn them away but there was no chance of that and their feet stirred up the mud and made waves which sent icy water trickling over the top of my gum boots and wetting the hem of my skirt. I finally managed to grasp hold of the stem of a water lily and pull it towards me. Just as it got close enough and as I was about to flip the big leaf over to look for snails, Muku's trunk slid around my hand, gently plucked the leaf off the stem and ate it. Reaching and pulling another water lily leaf towards me Muku repeated his performance. The third time Rundi was the thief, getting a firm grip on the leaf I was pulling towards me, she snatched it out of my fingers and pushed it into her mouth.

"Go away you two. Go on, push off!"

My words were wasted and the elephants stood like sentries, one on either side of me waiting for the next water lily. Realising I needed another plan; I found another clump of water lilies, pulled the whole thing to shore and dragged it out of the water. Rundi and Mundi didn't hesitate; they turned away from me and started feasting immediately. While they were occupied I moved to another spot to try again. At last I found a snail under a slimy leaf, carefully slid it off and put it in the bag on the damp cotton wool. One down a few dozen to go!

After what seemed like an awfully long time, I had collected about fifty snails and had become so absorbed in getting the job done that I hadn't noticed the elephants had finished their aperitif. Foolishly I had left the bag of snails on the ground. Bending over to search under another leaf I saw movement behind me, swung round to see an elephant. Muku delicately picked up my plastic bag of snails.

"Oh no Muku, not the snails, please!"

Muku had the prize and my words were useless. When I tried to get the bag of snails back from Muku he began to swing it slowly from side to side. I already knew in the pit of my stomach that this wasn't going to end well There wasn't a thing I could do except watch as Muku raised his trunk, delicately but firmly holding my bag of snails, and hit himself on the head with it repeatedly. Dismayed at the sight of all my hard work being smashed to a pulp I shouted at Muku who began reversing away from me before spreading his ears, lifting his tail and trumpeting.

Knowing that this was all just hot air and noise I finally managed to snatch the bag from him and clapping my hands I shouted at them both to go away. It was almost four o'clock by then and I had nothing to show for an afternoon's back breaking, smelly work except for a headache, a bad temper and a bag of slimy carcasses and broken shells.

Rundi and Muku stood a few metres away watching as I muttered and cursed. Wagging a finger at them I told them again to go away in a stern voice and went off to find another snail collecting spot. Rundi had the tip of her trunk in her mouth, looking as if she was sucking her thumb, and there was no doubt that my reprimand had worked as they both looked very chastened and sheepish. Coming on a group of undisturbed water lilies and reeds I hit the jackpot. The underneaths of the leaves were full of snails and I eagerly slid them off and straight into another sample bag. Glancing at my mud stained watch I saw that it was quarter to five and decided to call it a day and collected my things together. By then I had worked my way round to the other side of the dam and rather than trudge all the way back the way I'd come, I found a narrow place where the river came in and jumped across. I could see the elephants feeding in the shallow water some distance away and called out to them.

"Come on you two, let's go!"

As I stood in the thick dry grass waiting for the elephants, I shivered slightly. A cold wind had come up and as my damp skirt flapped against my knees all I wanted to do was go home and get into a hot bath.

"Come on Rundi!" I called again.

She had waded quite far into the water, possibly to find a clear stretch of un-muddied water to drink from. I noticed that the water was lapping against her belly. Rundi lifted her trunk out of the water, casually curled it back and squirted a load of water into her mouth. I called for the third time. Rundi aimed her trunk in my direction scented me and for some strange reason decided to walk through the water

Treating abscesses

Treating abscesses

Mud baths

Dust baths

Water squirting

Hand sucking

Mud and water

Walking with elephants

What are you eating?

Play mounting

Ear sucking

Playing in the sun

Horse cubes

Hose pipes

Appearance of tusks

Trunks entwined

Rundi　　　　　　　　*Muku*

Oscar, Ray, Simon

towards me instead of backtracking and going back the way she had come. I felt a bit anxious as she went deeper as I knew that somewhere in the dam was a deep sink hole, much too deep for her to walk through.

"No Rundi, go back!"

I turned and began to run through the grass parallel to the dam hoping that she would also change her direction and return to the shallows but it was too late, she was already in trouble. The dam had a very thick clay base and it was obvious from the way Rundi started to thrash around that she was stuck in the thick clinging mud. Horrified I watched helplessly as she tried to pull herself forward but made no progress at all. She lifted her trunk and trumpeted in a hitch pitched scream. She was well and truly stuck and as her weight settled into the mud, the water level rose higher on her belly. Rundi rumbled loudly and began to shake her head from side to side, clearly frustrated and angry.

She needed help! I dropped everything and ran back to the other side of the dam, leaping over the narrow gap across the river, stumbling in the dense grass and constantly losing my footing. I waded into the water behind her, calling her name repeatedly so that if she did try and move it would be backwards towards me and not further into the deep water. The more Rundi struggled the deeper she settled into the mud. When I reached her she rumbled at me and then growled and groaned; she was now clearly distressed.

I couldn't think what to do so for a minute or two I just stood next to her stroking her head and patting her while I tried to work out how to help her. I was scared and my heart was racing but at last I pulled myself together, plunged my arms under the water and tried to pull up one of her legs. By then I was almost up to my waist in water and stuck in the mud up to my knees. No matter how hard I struggled, I just couldn't get a firm grip around Rundi's leg and it didn't move at all. Rundi trumpeted wildly and then did something very silly. She laid her head down in the water as if she had given up. The water was thick with churned mud and when I finally managed to get my arms under her jaw and lift her head out of the water, she was coated in mud. She snorted runny mud out of her trunk and I realised that the inside of her nose must have been lined with the stuff. I was desperate to help free Rundi and beginning to think that if I didn't do something fast she was going to drown right in front of me, almost in my arms.

I frantically looked around for something which could help me drag this 400 kg elephant out of the mud. Alone, with no vehicle, radio or means of communication; stuck in the mud; almost dark: things couldn't have been much worse. Suddenly out of nowhere Joçam appeared. I don't think I'd ever been so pleased to see him. Joçam was a Malawian, one of the hardest workers I had ever encountered. If you asked Joçam to dig a hole he excavated a well. He ran everywhere, did everything at double speed and didn't mix much with the other workers. His grasp of English was almost non-existent and he didn't seem to understand much Shona either so it was incredibly difficult to communicate with him. He also had the most infuriating habit of smiling at everything, a habit which was normally funny, but not today.

So there I was, standing in the dam, water over my waist and almost thigh deep in soft, cold mud. I could feel the mud in my boots and in my underpants and tried not to think about the crabs and other multiple legged creatures and other biting, stinging, slimy, slippery things that must be all around me. Joçam was walking parallel to the dam but was on the outside of the game fence and obviously on his way home.

"Joçam, help me!" I screamed out, waving my arms frantically.

Joçam stopped walking and very politely, predictably, lifted his hat and called out probably the only phrase he knew: "Good Night!"

"No! No! Help me Joçam. Rundi is stuck!"

Again Joçam lifted his hat and smiled but didn't move.

"Help me Joçam, please, help me. Come!" I beckoned to him, waving my arms, gesturing repeatedly for him to come. Still he didn't move and a litany of uncharitable things went through my mind; couldn't he see we needed help? Did he really think I was fully clothed and waist deep in the dam at 5pm for the fun of it?

Again I called: "Help me Joçam! Please come!" I couldn't think of what else to say but at last I seemed to have got through to him and I breathed a sigh of relief to see him starting to climb up the two and a half metre high diamond mesh fence.

With help finally on the way I again put my arms under Rundi's trunk which had fallen into the water with only the tip exposed. I lifted her trunk up; it was heavy and a dead weight in my arms. I talked to Rundi all the time and she watched me constantly, her big brown eyes staring into mine. My tears were very close so I looked away. I wasn't going to let this baby elephant drown.

Joçam finally got to the top of fence, over and down on the inside. Without hesitating he sploshed into the water and waded out to where we were, soon slowed down by the thick mud sucking on his legs.

"Oh thank you Joçam, thank you!" I whispered.

Pointing to Rundi's backside, I gestured to Joçam to try and push her free of the thick mud.

"Push!" I implored and Joçam was in his element; this was exactly what he was best at: hard physical exertion. It was as an impossible task: aside from her trunk there was nothing to hold on to and Rundi seemed to have given up or was totally exhausted and she just didn't or couldn't help at all. Rundi was almost laying in the mess of filthy water and clinging mud and looked close to being completely submerged. Her breathing was fast and shallow and she moaned softly, her eyes white and rolling, big with fear and helplessness.

All this time Muku had obviously been confused and frustrated, rushing backwards and forwards along the bank of the dam, trumpeting, rumbling and defecating everywhere. Suddenly he came splashing into the dam, ploughing through the mud, making more as he went, before stopping next to us. It was the most endearing thing to see him gently sniffing and touching Rundi's eyes, head and trunk with the tip of his trunk and then he started pushing against her with his head. A real disaster seemed imminent as Muku's pushing made Rundi's stance even worse and she sank even lower into the mud. It was impossible to try and get Muku to go away but Rundi did try and help herself for a moment: she struggled weakly when, unbelievably, Muku put his whole head under water and tried to raise Rundi's head.

Nothing seemed to be helping and the more Muku pushed, the weaker Rundi got; her trunk slipped out of my hands and into the water and she gasped weakly and rolled her eyes as I snatched it back up out of the water. Rundi was now obviously too weak to even hold her own trunk out of the water.

I knew with certainty that Rundi was going to drown if we didn't do something fast; stopping Muku became the priority. I shouted at him and tried to push him away but he trumpeted loudly and butted into me. The only thing keeping me upright was the mud my legs were stuck in and for a moment I thought if I wasn't careful I might be the one who would drown here today if Muku head butted me again.

Completely wet and with one elephant drowning and the other trying to help but making things worse, Joçam suddenly splashed past me out of the water and came back with a thick length of old bamboo that had been lying near the fence. He positioned the bamboo lengthways behind Rundi's backside and began to push. As I felt the slightest movement I laid Rundi's trunk over my shoulder, tilted my head sideways to keep it out of the water, bent down, plunged my arms and chest into the water and tugged at one of her front legs, trying to pull it up out of the mud. Muku seemed to get the idea and joined in the pushing until we all felt Rundi move forward slightly. I looked up at Joçam and we both grinned wildly: the elephant's movement gave us renewed vigour in what had seemed an impossible task. Muku too must have felt Rundi move slightly and he kept pushing against her backside with his forehead.

With combined pulling and pushing we shouted for joy when one foot came free, the release giving Rundi the momentum she so desperately needed to struggle forward one step. After the first two steps we could feel Rundi's freedom in our grasp. Muku and Joçam pushed on Rundi's backside, I pulled on her leg and Rundi forced her weight forwards and then at last we were able to turn her: away from deep water and to the left of the treacherous mud. Rundi joined in, finally able to use her own strength to break free of the mud and get a firmer base under foot. One step, two and then more as the mud and water got shallower. Rundi struggled forwards and at last got to the shore.

Joçam and I stood at the water's edge; what a state we were in: both soaked from head to foot, clothes filthy, hair and faces spattered with slime and grime; legs, boots and shoes thickly plastered in mud. We shivered from cold and shock. Wiping my hands on the grass I rescued my cigarettes from the bag I had thrown down on the ground before launching into the dam, eventually got my hands to stop shaking enough to light two, passing one to Joçam . That had been a close call to disaster and tragedy. Rundi would have drowned if Joçam hadn't come past when he did. There was no doubt in my mind that I just didn't have the physical strength to have done it on my own; Joçam had saved Rundi's life.

Rundi stood at the edge of the dam, her head down, legs shaking, visibly shivering. Her breathing was fast and shallow. I'm not sure who was more shaken from the experience, the people or the elephants but we made our way slowly back to the platform. I immediately attached a hosepipe to the tap and gently washed Rundi down while Joçam squelched his way off to Oscar's cottage for help. By the time Joçam returned with Oscar, Simon and Ray, I had washed all the mud off Rundi and Muku had also had a good shower too: playing more than being rinsed down. In his mixture of Malawian, Shona, English and sign language Joçam explained to the others what had happened. It was a wondrous pantomime to watch, especially the mime about him and the bamboo log for leverage and me ducking under water to push and pull on Rundi's legs, her trunk thrown over my shoulder.

Simon went to get empty buckets, Raymond to get a special extra bucket of milk and porridge and Oscar to bring a sack of vegetables. Like an anxious mother Simon talked quietly to Rundi, whispering and murmuring while gently holding her trunk into a bucket of water trying to encourage her to flush out her trunk in the clean water.

Rundi sucked up some water and immediately squirted it back out and it was full of mud. Coaxing and cajoling we managed to get her to suck and rinse her trunk twice more but she was clearly exhausted. Her body was racked with shivering, her trunk limp and floppy and she looked very forlorn. Shock was obviously setting in and for the first time ever we had a struggle getting her to finish her bucket of milk and porridge. Rundi sucked on the milk mixture slowly, her trunk shaking as she lifted it to tip the contents into her mouth. Ray and Oscar had to block Muku from barging in and sharing Rundi's milk, he had finished his very rapidly and wasn't showing any signs of shock. When she had finished her milk I stroked Rundi behind her ear and tears stung my eyes when she rumbled softly at me in response; we had nearly lost her. The two elephants were led into their stable under the platform and lay down next to each other in their deep bed of hay. Simon would keep an eye on them now and so Joçam and I went our separate ways after prolonged handshakes and back slapping: a hot shower was beckoning.

Early the next morning I went straight to the elephants. They had both emerged from their deep hay bed and were feeding on the remnants of the vegetable pile. Scattering a pile of cubes I stood watching them, looking for anything unusual after the trauma of twelve hours ago. Rundi seemed quite lethargic, not feeding with her usual voracity and her trunk was definitely more floppy than usual. She was incredibly affectionate towards me, rumbling repeatedly, putting my hand into her mouth, touching my face with the tip of her trunk or just laying it on my hair. Her behaviour towards me was very moving and Muku was just Muku: contented, friendly, stuffing food into his mouth, showing no obvious ill effect of the late afternoon episode in the deep mud. When Simon arrived he took the pair off on their usual early morning walk, taking it very slowly, not going far and staying well away from the dam where the churned up mud gouged with Rundi's deep tracks would be a death trap until it dried up. I increased the elephants' normal daily ration of cubes and arranged that Rundi would be given milk and porridge morning and afternoon for the next week until she had completely recovered from being stuck in the mud.

EIGHT

....

For about a week after she'd been stuck in the mud Rundi was much
quieter than usual. She spent long periods of time just standing at
the platform or sleeping in the sun, not venturing out into the game
park as usual. The shock of the ordeal of being stuck in the mud had
clearly affected her and the near drowning had also given me a big
fright. I couldn't understand why Rundi had got stuck in the first place
and why Muku hadn't also got stuck; he was heavier than her and had
followed her exact route into the dam and then stood right next to her
as we tried to extricate her but he hadn't got stuck. Perhaps it was just
a combination of Rundi's height, the length of her legs and her being
physically weaker than Muku and therefore just unable to pull herself
out of the mud. If the water in the dam had been deeper there probably
wouldn't have been a problem at all.

I'd never seen Rundi or Muku swim but elephants are well known
for their ability in water. Ian and I had witnessed one elephant
swimming a distance of over six kilometres between two islands on
Lake Kariba. Out boating one day we had spotted something black in
the water and thinking it was the tip of a submerged tree, slowed down
to navigate around the obstacle. A closer look showed the black object
to actually be the tip of a submerged elephant's trunk, being used as a
snorkel! Keeping our distance so as not to accidentally hit the elephant

we had watched with binoculars as the snorkel moved away. Soon it was impossible to see the tip of the elephant's trunk until after some time we saw it, emerging out of the water as a full grown elephant onto the shores of Long Island. This was one of scores of sightings of elephants swimming there, the most famous being when Lake Kariba was being constructed and water started to flood the land. Elephants were often seen swimming from what had become Fothergill Island all the way to Andora Harbour, a distance of twenty two kilometres.

Rundi's close encounter in the dam didn't appear to have a long term effect on her but both she and Muku avoided the side of the dam where the incident had taken place. It didn't deter their love of mud however and it wasn't long before she and Muku were happily back mud bathing which was a regular occurrence for them.

The process always started with having a drink. Standing side by side the two elephants would suck up some water, lift their heads and tip the contents of their trunks into their mouths. Muku often started the mud bath ritual and the signal seemed to be when he swished his trunk rapidly from side to side in the water. After stirring up the water Muku would suck up a trunk full and start squirting himself. Just like putting a finger over the end of a hosepipe, he was able to control the amount and pressure of water being released. By squeezing the tips of the trunk together, or prehensile lips as they are called, the elephants could get the water to come out of their trunks in a thin jet and then the spraying began: between the front legs, under the belly, on their backs and hind legs, on top of their heads. It wasn't long before they were both fully engrossed in showering; ears were spread out and again and again trunk-full's of water were squirted all over their bodies.

Still standing side by side and often with their heads touching, the pair would then liberally cover themselves in mud, scooping it up in the curves of their trunks and then flicking and throwing it over their heads, along their sides and between their legs. Then, as if they couldn't resist for another moment, they would suddenly collapse onto their knees and flop down into the mud. On their sides, legs stretched out, the elephants squirted more mud onto themselves and wriggled and squirmed in the cool mess until they had made a comfortable hollow for themselves in the sticky red mud. Sometimes Rundi and Muku would lie partially on top of each other or entwine their trunks over each other and wallow in the mud for as long as half an hour with their skin completely coated in mud. Eventually when one or the other elephant, usually Rundi, let out a long low rumble, they would slip and slide and struggle back up onto their feet. The ritual always ended with the elephants finding a clear stretch of water where they would flush the mud out of their trunks and have a last drink before proceeding to the second half of the ritual, the dust bath.

Rundi and Muku had mud bath locations at the pan in front of the platform, at the lower dam where Rundi had been so close to drowning and at a site we called the Poison Quarry. The quarry had once been a gravel extraction pit for road works and later became a dumping site before the establishment of the Mukuvisi Woodlands and the erection of the fence. Volunteers had cleared all the litter out of the quarry and found many drums of chemicals and other toxic waste in the process; waste which had contaminated the soil and left the quarry devoid of most vegetation: a red, stony waste ground. Not so when elephants came to the Woodlands! In the rainy season the runoff would channel water down the slopes into the Quarry and a substantial pool gathered in the bottom; this became a favourite mud bathing spot.

Whenever the elephants accompanied members of the game committee on a patrol, the Poison Quarry was always a favourite stopping point. There were a lot of Mahobohobo trees (*Uapaca kirkiana*) in the area and the succulent orange fruits were favourites with both people and elephants. Sitting on one of the high stony piles around the quarry eating the sweet orange fruits and taking a break during a long hot patrol, the elephants never failed to entertain themselves and us. Beth and Pete Taylor came back a few times looking like they'd been dragged through a hedge backwards. What had happened was something Pete remembered three decades later:

"During the rains when the Poison Quarry filled up and the high sides turned into mud slides, Mom and I, on three different occasions, were pushed down with 600 kg of baby elephant very close behind. They just loved the muddy mess after a few times down, nothing like a mud pack. And Mom and I looked much the same."

Ian and I also often returned from walking with the elephants looking very second hand after an encounter at the mud bath. Once they were completely covered in red mud if we'd been at the Quarry or black mud if we'd been at the lower dam, Rundi and Muku always came and greeted, sniffed and rubbed up against us afterwards, leaving their muddy imprints all over us.

After their mud bath, Rundi and Muku walked until they came to a well used trampled site where the sand was soft and then the dust bath began. Squeezing the tip of the trunk closed and shaping a little curved scoop, they would lift soft sand up and tip it over their heads. Then they threw sand over their backs, between their legs and wherever else it would stick. Rundi would get down on her front knees, trunk carefully tucked under her chin, backside sticking up in their air, and she would grind her forehead into the sand as if itching or scratching something irritating her under the skin. Next Muku sank down onto all fours in a kneeling position and would flap his ears while continually throwing sand over his head. After about ten minutes the elephants would get up and carry on walking, both looking very peculiar with patches of dry, cracked mud all over their bodies and a little line of sand always left on top of their heads and along the ridge of their spines.

The skin of an elephant is extremely thick and creased; three to four centimetres thick on their legs, forehead, trunk and back. The skin of an adult bull elephant weighs around 418 kg and I guessed that Rundi and Muku's skin probably weighed about 60 kg, allowing an extra 5 kg in the form of wet mud! Their mud and dust bath routine was a way of coating their skin to protect them from insects and scratches although they only seemed to be troubled by large biting flies on their backs during the hottest months of summer. That didn't stop them from having mud and dust baths all year round, regardless of the seasons.

Regardless of the thickness of their skin or how much mud they had plastered on themselves, Rundi and Muku were still not immune from the countless missiles that were thrown at them all the time. We had put up notices everywhere:

'People throwing objects at the crocodiles will be asked to retrieve them!'

'Do not feed the squirrels!'

'Do not feed the animals!'

'No food to be taken into the game area!'

'Leave nothing but footprints, take nothing but photographs!'

These were just some of the signs we put up at the various animal viewing sites around the woodlands but mostly they were ignored. We regularly found stones, sticks, pieces of brick, tins and drink bottles in the crocodile enclosure. From the car park all the way down to the viewing platform, collecting litter was a daily necessity: cigarette ends, crisp packets, sweet papers, plastic bags: it never ended. The elephants were not ignored when it came to the problem either as people threw all sorts of missiles at them ranging from lit cigarettes to glass bottles: anything to get a reaction from them or to get that much sought after photo opportunity. People always wanted 'action' shots of animals doing things: eating, drinking, fighting, mating: something exciting. People wanted to see animals being active and if it meant throwing things at them to achieve their objective, that's what they'd do. It didn't seem to register with most visitors that by throwing things at the elephants or feeding them hazardous litter or left over picnic food they were creating a problem that invariably led to an animal dying or having to be removed. There was nothing more infuriating than seeing Rundi and Muku carrying around plastic bags or with empty bottles in their trunks and it soon led to a real problem with Muku.

Picking up rubbish became an obsession with Muku and if anything was thrown over the platform he would retrieve it. He would eat it, suck it, carry it around or put it on his head. Taking a group of tourists into the game park on a safari one day, the guide came back to relate Muku's latest behaviour. A young couple were among the group and the woman was carrying an ice cream cone. The guide didn't notice that someone had food and, as was the usual routine, he stopped just inside the gate to explain the layout of the Woodlands and to give people a chance to see the elephants. Without any coaxing at all Rundi and Muku sauntered over to the group. Rundi made straight for the guide and immediately started sucking on his hand, causing guests to immediately start taking photos; this was most definitely in the category of unusual photographs. Meanwhile in the background Muku had his heart set on getting the ice cream which the guide only noticed when there was a single, high-pitched scream.

The young woman stood with her arm above her head, the ice cream inevitably turning to liquid and starting to drip down her arm, while Muku made determined efforts to get the prize from her elevated hand. Muku wrapped his trunk around the woman's raised arm and was trying to pull her hand down. The more she tried to resist, the more determined Muku became and when the guide came over and tried to push Muku away, the elephant didn't move but rumbled loudly; it was quite clear that he wasn't going anywhere until he got that ice cream. Alone with a dozen tourists and two elephants, the guide assessed the situation and not knowing what else to do, told the woman to forfeit the ice cream. Frightened and embarrassed the woman lowered her arm and ever so gently Muku took her ice cream and put it in his mouth accompanied by a barrage of clicking cameras from all directions. The ice cream was gone in a second and Muku then carefully sniffed the woman all over her head and face with the tip of his trunk. The woman was embarrassed but the guide was relieved, knowing how quickly and easily this funny encounter could have turned nasty.

Muku was definitely an elephant worthy of the psychiatrist's couch. He did the strangest things and seemed to take particular pleasure in carrying things. Muku would often walk for considerable distances carrying something he had found: a plastic bag, stick or even a piece of string from a feed sack. Muku particularly loved walking sticks and one guide coming back after leading a safari leant tiredly against the kiosk counter.

"Tired?" I asked sympathetically.

"Mmm, and my knee's killing me," George replied, rubbing the affected area

"Did you forget your stick today?" I knew George always carried a stout walking stick when he took guests around the game park. It doubled up as walking aid, a weapon if needed and something with which he could flip over stones or branches to perhaps expose a creature hidden underneath such as a spider, scorpion, centipede or snake.

"No, that damn Muku took it off me and has still got it now! He just wouldn't give it back. I picked up another stick as we went round on the tour but it didn't give me the support I'm used to."

Muku had met the safari group when they went in the gate of the game park, made a beeline for George and relieved him of his sturdy, polished walking stick almost immediately. Leaving George having tea under the shade of the Lucky Bean tree at the kiosk, I went straight to the platform and looked down on the elephants. They were looking quite angelic, standing side by side in the sun, heads together, eyes heavy with sleep. The stolen walking stick was laying on the ground a few metres away. Armed with a handful of cubes I went down from the platform, unlocked the gate and strolled over to the elephants. Just as I had guessed he would, Muku immediately walked to where the walking stick lay, picked it up and held it on top of his head, his pink mouth slightly open, looking for all the world as if he was laughing at me. I ignored Muku completely, walked past him to Rundi, and gave her some cubes, stroked her behind the ears and we rumbled at each other.

Watching Muku out of the corner of my eye I knew he wouldn't be able to resist joining in and sure enough he came over to us, still holding the stick on his head. Casually I dropped a few cubes on the ground. Yet again he couldn't resist and immediately let go of the walking stick which clattered to the ground and he began picking up cubes instead. Casually, without any fuss, I bent down, picked up George's walking stick and beat a hasty retreat. Turning to lock the gate on my way out I saw Muku watching me, his trunk raised, smelling the air in my direction. The much loved, smoothly worn stick would never be the same again: covered in dry saliva and mud, the rubber foot was gone and three deep white scratches, made by Muku's teeth, scarred its beautiful grain. Despite its deplorable state, George was delighted at the return of his cherished stick which now had its own tale to tell: it bore the marks of an elephant.

Rundi and Muku both had a very keen sense of smell and were constantly sniffing the wind to find out who or what was around. They smelled all the visitors who came into the game park; sometimes it was a cursory sniff and other times it was the whole works. As soon as the gate into the park opened, trunks would come up to sniff the wind. Ears opened and flapped and then they would trundle over, waving their trunks in front of them. If it was someone they were not familiar with, a tip to toe investigative sniffing session often followed. Usually starting at the feet, the trunk was held a few millimetres away and the person would be minutely checked out. Shoes were often of particular interest:

a million squashed smells waiting to be identified and if something special was found, the elephants would touch all round the edges of the shoe with the tip of their trunks. They would even curl their trunk around a leg and try and lift a person's foot off the ground or nudge it with their own foot so they could get a better smell underneath. Many guests would hold on to me, hopping on one foot and giggling hysterically as the soles of their shoes were sniffed avidly.

Once the feet were inspected the trunk would move up the legs, over the skirt or trousers or, on one memorably embarrassing occasion, under a woman's skirt. She went redder and redder as Muku repeatedly put his trunk under her skirt and sniffed around. The more embarrassed she got, the more the other guests laughed and despite all my attempts to get Muku out of her skirt, he repeatedly bumped me away and resumed his under-skirt investigation until he was satisfied. Whilst Muku had a great curiosity for the soles of shoes and underwear, Rundi was obsessed with smelling hair. My hair was always slightly more wild than normal and permanently sticky with saliva after a session with Rundi. At first she would sniff very carefully all over your head and then she'd rest the lower part of her trunk on your head and bury the tip of her trunk in your hair. It was an amazing sensation and quite emotional too as I interpreted this and other tactile behaviour from both her and Muku as a form of recognition, even acceptance into their herd.

The elephant's sense of smell seemed to be getting stronger as they grew up. There were times when a particular smell fascinated them for inexplicable reasons, one of which was each other's droppings. They would sniff each other's newly deposited droppings very closely, placing the tip of the trunk just above the hot manure, inhaling the smell and then lifted up the trunk up and blew the smell into their mouth. Tasting the smell was the best way I could find to describe this amazing behaviour but I had no idea why they did it. Sometimes tasting the smell went a step further and Rundi and Muku actually ate each other's droppings.

"No they aren't starving!" I would have to tell visitors again and again when they asked if the elephants were eating each other's faeces because they weren't getting enough food.

Trying to understand why they did this, I turned to the reference books. What I wouldn't have given to have the internet and Google back in the 1980s, not to mention email, cell phones or any of the other forms of communication and access to information that would change the world beyond all recognition in a few years time. Books I consulted said scientists believed that by eating their own (or their parents) faeces, a young elephant established micro-organisms in its stomach which were essential for its own digestion. I knew that elephants have a simple stomach and poor digestion which is why they have to eat so much but it took close physical inspection of their dung to see which items they ate didn't break down at all. Often after they'd been eating supplementary feed containing maize, the kernels came through completely untouched; the same applied to pumpkins, butternuts and other vegetables with hard seeds. It even applied to tomato seeds as I had discovered a couple of months before.

It had been the time of year when the whole Woodland abounded with bright yellow butterflies which, for some unknown reason, found something to their liking in freshly laid elephant dung, around which they clustered and fluttered providing a beautiful spectacle. The butterflies seemed to be feeding on something in the dung but it was impossible to identify what it was. The piles of elephant dung provided a great deal of humour in the days when it was hot, humid and, if we were lucky, there was rain too. The droppings were filled with germinating seedlings of pumpkins and tomatoes; the seedlings crowding their way out of the dung like too many prickles on a hedgehog, pushing out in all directions, competing for space and nourishment, The majority of the seedlings would not survive, becoming either drowned in the rain or scorched in the sun, but one or two managed to become established on the small island at the pan in front of the platform. Soon a large and spreading pumpkin plant began to creep across the ground and later produced six very large fruits, the progress of which was jealously guarded by Oscar, who laid claim to them the moment they were ripe enough to harvest.

The thought of elephant dung benefitting the very people who cared for Rundi and Muku was rewarding but it wasn't only people who gained from their excretions. We often saw other animals, particularly small antelope and birds picking through elephant droppings and selecting titbits to eat.

Hard as I tried to accept the reality of Rundi and Muku eating each other's droppings, I did find it a most unpleasant habit and, to make matters worse, the fresher the droppings were, the more appealing the faeces seemed to be. It was not amusing to be sniffed and touched by an elephant with wet faeces on its trunk. It was even less amusing when it happened to someone who had paid to go on a safari only to discover that the experience started out by being dabbed with wet elephant faeces by an elephant! As Rundi and Muku grew in, and thankfully out, of this habit, I often wished I could get the elephants to dab faeces onto the people who insisted on feeding them plastic bags or lit cigarettes or who poked them with sticks and threw stones at them to get an action photograph.

NINE

....

The first winter that Rundi and Muku spent at the Woodlands was
a very hard one. It followed a particularly tough drought which
had left the vegetation much sparser than normal, increasing the
competition for the little vegetation that was available. The mornings
through May and June were bitterly cold and always began with a thick
frost which killed the last remnants of goodness in the grazing. An icy
wind was my constant companion on daily patrols in the game park
and I became increasingly worried about the elephants who found less
and less to eat as we walked. Dusk comes early in winter and when I
went home every evening at five, the elephants could no longer be seen
grazing in the open grassland, they just went to their stable under the
platform and didn't emerge until the sun was well up the next day.

The new ritual for the time of year was daily winter feeding, the
bulk of which was donated by stockfeed company Agrifoods and other
well wishers. Winter feed consisted of a high protein, low urea feed,
in the form of mash or pellets; a mineral lick which was high in salt,
phosphorous and molasses and a home-made silage made from lucerne
and mixed with hay, ground nut hay, oil and cotton seed husks. The
elephants received an increase in the amount of porridge they got in
their milk every day, double the daily ration of cubes and triple the
amount of vegetables. A new fruit and vegetable donation had been

sourced by Terry Fallon and we were delighted to get 30 kg of fresh produce from Favco just a few hundred metres down the Transtobac Road. Sourcing the feed, finding donors, taking delivery, mixing and storing all this extra food for the winter programme took a lot of time and hard work and as usual wasn't made any easier by the predictable barrage of complaints from the armchair critics.

"Let nature take care of her own," they would say, or "survival of the fittest."

Their sentiments drove me mad! It was man and not nature that had erected the fence and man, not nature that had brought in species from many hundreds of kilometres away and put them in an area a fraction of the size of their normal territorial range.

"When man erects a fence and fills the area with animals he must either feed them or take the wire down, particularly in years when nature brings drought or fire," was my response. Luckily my sentiments were shared by Peter Brookes Ball, the Chairman of the Mukuvisi Woodlands at the time and so I counted animals and consulted carrying capacity reports compiled by University of Zimbabwe graduates.

I spent hours at my desk calculating the proportions: the weight and composition of the ingredients, the weights and numbers of animals and how many kgs of supplementary food they would need to maintain their condition and get through winter. In the evenings I went over all my lists and calculations and instead of making grocery shopping lists for home, I was writing down how many drums of molasses or bales of hay would be needed for the animals! I finally came up with a formula of the proportions of ingredients and how much to give every day so that it would last five months before the rains and green grass returned.

As truck loads of stockefeed rumbled in, the elephants screamed, trumpeted, put their tails out and ran away; their only knowledge of trucks came from their capture and being taken away from their herds; they didn't know anything good came in vehicles. Soon the storeroom under the platform was full of fifty kg sacks of food along with salt and mineral blocks. This was the only place that was dry and secure and we packed it to the rafters.

Terry Fallon was invaluable in co-ordinating this huge task, arranging transport and deliveries of the bulkier ingredients such as hay, silage and oil seed husks which went straight to the boma. Huge piles of hay and lucerne, loosely baled and badly tied, collapsed into mountains of jumble; truck loads of oil seed husks donated by Olivine Industries were dumped in gigantic piles; drums of molasses, filthy and sticky, completed the ingredients and as the trucks left, the elephants sniffed long and hard in the direction of five months worth of feed.

As we needed them, the required quantities of ingredients were moved from the storeroom to the boma in wheelbarrows, well away from the elephants. Luckily the boma was empty of animals at the time so we laid big sheets of tin on the ground where we could mix the winter feed.

Simon and I set out for the boma to mix the food for the animals' first winter meal. Despite the cool weather, this was a hot, dusty, dirty job and it took us an hour and half to measure, mix, bag and load the feed onto wheelbarrows. With aching, bent-over backs, Simon and I pushed the banquet out of the boma, across the dry river bed and up into the grassland in the vlei in front of the platform. We spread the food out in piles so that all the animals would be able to get to it and then stood back to look at our handiwork. Suddenly Simon's face broke into a wide, beaming grin.

"They have come!" he announced, pointing to the grey lumps moving steadily closer.

"Damn!" I exclaimed. "Quickly Simon, put your cubes into the wheelbarrow and let's move right away from here."

We had planned all this very carefully. The feed we had mixed and put out in piles in the grassland was not for the elephants, it was for the other animals: zebra, eland, wildebeest, tsessebe, impala and other smaller, shyer species such as duiker and steenbuck. Thankfully it didn't take too much persuading to get the elephants to follow Simon and the wheelbarrow; the smell of cubes was obviously too much to resist. They did look funny running alongside Simon, their backsides wobbling in their loose, baggy skin, ears flapping and trunks desperately trying to snatch the cubes which bounced up and down in the barrow as Simon ran over bumpy, uneven ground. Simon was back at the platform long before me and when I arrived we tipped out the elephants' new daily ration: four, fifty kg sacks of vegetables.

Aside from the countless sacks of free vegetables we collected every day from Honeydew Farm, a new source came to help us keep the animals alive through winter. Stuart Pringle, the owner of a very popular take-away restaurant, the Hamburger Hut, in Newlands shopping centre, a few kilometres from the Mukuvisi Woodlands, offered to help with vegetable off-cuts from the restaurant. Every day a car arrived with large plastic dustbins crammed full of leftovers and trimmings: sliced tomato, onion rings, lettuce, chunks of pineapple, carrot rings, cucumber circles, mushrooms, coleslaw and fruit salad. This was heaven, an invaluable gift which kept all our tortoises in prime condition and left a lot to add to the elephants' never ending buffet table. You could almost see the elephants smiling when you arrived with the Hamburger Hut off-cuts and often there were streams of silver drool hanging and dripping from the corners of their mouths before you'd even finished putting the feast out for them.

"Aah, this would be good for customers," said a voice from behind me and there was Oscar. We often met at the platform at the end of the day and while Oscar rolled and then smoked one of his smelly home-made cigarettes, we would look out into the evening and find a bit of peace from the beauty at our feet that we toiled so hard to achieve every day.

"Oscar, you know how much trouble it would cause if our tourists saw the animals eating supplementary feed?"

"Yes, some wouldn't be happy, but look how close the animals are. The tourists would be able to see everything so well, and take very good photographs. "

"Well, if the tourists come late in the afternoon and see this then that's OK but with all the Board members arguing about what's natural and what's not, I'm not going to advertise this winter feeding Oscar."

We stayed for a while longer watching as animals came and went to the piles of supplementary feed laid out in the grassland. Directly below us in front of the platform Rundi and Muku crunched contentedly and noisily on cabbage leaves, chunks of pumpkin and delicately sliced onion rings with the odd treasures of a piece of apple, banana and pineapple for their sweet tooth. Neither of us knew that as times and Board members changed in years to come, our winter supplementary feeding programme would become a major highlight for the Woodlands and a huge draw card for tourists, providing much needed revenue from visitors.

By the end of the first week Simon and I had the feeding down to a fine art. I gave different feeds on alternate days: one day the animals had the balanced granular supplementary feed mixed with cotton seed husks and the next day we mixed hay, lucerne and cotton seed husks and sprayed it with molasses. This was how I had planned to stretch the food out over five months and everything worked like clockwork until the elephants broke into the boma and raided the pantry.

Arriving at work at seven thirty in the morning I was met at the office door by four very worried faces. Oscar, Ray, Simon and Joçam stood quietly aside as I went into the office before slowly trooping in behind me. I sat down at my desk and looked up, waiting for someone to spill the beans. At last Oscar broke the silence.

"We are very sorry!"

I frowned but said nothing, waiting for him to carry on.

"It's Muku, he's very sick."

I didn't waste a second and headed straight for the game viewing platform, followed closely by all the workers. Even with the brisk walking, I shivered as I reached the gate and my frozen fingers struggled with the padlock. As soon as I saw Muku I could see there was a big problem. He paced restlessly, continually flapping his ears and swinging his trunk rapidly from side to side. At first I thought it was colic which I'd seen before but Muku didn't look bloated and swollen with gas. When he held his tail straight out expelled a jet of very watery diarrhoea, I knew this wasn't bloat. Muku bellowed, clearly in pain, before resuming his pacing and ear flapping. He showed no interest in me at all and instead of the usual rumbled greeting and face sniffing, Muku groaned and paced. Going a little closer I frowned and picked a scrap of fluff off his back. Holding it in my open, shivering hand, I turned to Oscar.

"They've broken into the boma. Look, its cotton seed. Muku's been gorging on the winter feed."

Oscar sent the others to the boma while we stood watching Muku pacing, bellowing and squirting diarrhoea. Suddenly it came to me.

"Bananas! We must find bananas Oscar; plenty of them and feed them to Muku."

"Bananas! Why should we give him more food when he's been eating all night?"

As soon as he said that, I knew that Oscar knew the elephants had been feasting in the boma all night; in fact I'd bet that he hadn't found them at the platform when he came to open up this morning because they were probably still in the boma. I didn't query my theory because I needed to help Muku fast.

"We need bananas Oscar! Bananas stop diarrhoea. I'll go and find some now, meantime can you all get on to fixing the boma gates immediately. I suppose they did break the boma gates and not the fence?" Oscar didn't answer and I rushed off to buy bananas for an elephant.

Standing in the queue at the cafe holding about two dozen bananas I smiled when someone raised their eyes at my armful of bananas. Should I say they weren't for me but for my elephant, I wondered? I didn't!

As soon as I got back to the Woodlands I immediately fed Muku a dozen of the bananas. Both of the elephants usually loved bananas, the riper the better, and ate them skin and all but Muku wasn't at all keen after his feeding orgy of the night before. Stroking, rumbling and talking to him, I got him to eat some of the bananas and then coaxed him to dip his trunk into a bucket of water to get him drinking. Rundi was nervous and kept sniffing Muku and the diarrhoea piles and trying to suck my hand.

Leaving Muku to digest the first dozen bananas and hopefully calm down, I went to the boma to assess the damage. The crime scene told the whole story very clearly. Rundi and Muku had obviously been in the boma for most of the night judging by the mess and piles of dung everywhere. The cotton seed mountain had been considerably flattened, hay and lucerne were scattered everywhere. Three of the red, two hundred litre drums of molasses had been knocked over and rolled around a bit but luckily, due to their tight fitting plugs, they hadn't leaked, just got dented. The real damage and undoubtedly the cause of the diarrhoea, was the mess in the stack of bags which contained the cubes. A new delivery of stock feed had come a few days before and we'd moved some of the bags of cubes to the boma to make room in the storeroom. It was the bags of cubes that had done the damage. Two bags had been opened, the hessian no match for a determined elephant. It looked like at least 30–40 kg of cubes were gone, three times more than Muku usually had over a full day. What Muku had been given during the day plus what he'd stolen over night, it was no wonder he wasn't feeling well; this elephant had made a real pig of himself.

We couldn't understand why Rundi wasn't affected; perhaps Muku had gone to the cubes alone while Rundi was busy tossing cotton seed and scattering lucerne and hay or perhaps she'd tried to join Muku and he had butted and bullied her away from the cubes? Whatever had gone on here in the dead of night I was just thankful that Rundi wasn't in pain and squirting diarrhoea everywhere this morning. She was still smaller and thinner than Muku and it was a constant fight to keep her strong and healthy. It took Oscar and his team the best part of the morning to clear up the mess in the boma and re-stack all the food. Once that was done the next job was fixing the gate that Rundi and Muku had bashed and battered to get into the boma the night before. After much hammering, banging and wire tying the job was done. I fitted a new chain and padlock on the boma gates and our precious winter feed was secure again.

Muku didn't get any more cubes that day; bananas were on his menu and trips to the cafe were a repeated chore for me. Four or five dozen bananas later Muku stopped pacing and the diarrhoea dried up. The major disadvantage of the elephants' night time raid on the pantry was that now they knew where the food was they would surely be back. Despite all the repairs and the new padlock, I had all the bags of cubes moved to another storeroom; it was inconvenient as it meant double carrying but better to be safe than sorry. At least now if the elephants got back into the boma they could only gorge themselves on hay, dry lucerne and cotton seed husks which were all roughage, leaving little chance of diarrhoea. The whole incident reminded me that despite their size these two elephants were still babies and we needed to have eyes in the back of our heads to keep them strong and healthy.

As the shortest day of the year arrived, winter was evident everywhere. All the deciduous trees were completely bare and there wasn't a hint of green anywhere in the grass. Even with all the feed we were putting out every day, animals in the game park were getting noticeably leaner. They began coming closer and closer to the feeding area in the vlei above the pan and spending much of the day there, or just in the tree line nearby, waiting for the food to be put out. On one of those cold, windy, wintery days I received an over-supply of cabbages, far more than the elephants needed, so I carried a couple of bags out into the vlei and put piles of cabbages leaves on the grass. Not all the animals found cabbages palatable but the eland did. Soon after this they started coming right down to the platform, something they had never done before, and began challenging the elephants for cabbage leaves. It wasn't long before there was a showdown.

The elephants were extremely protective and defensive of the area that was their feeding and sleeping territory at the platform. They were even-tempered when people entered their domain but most definitely did not extend this invitation to any of the animals, or even birds, in the area. Both Rundi and Muku would chase birds which came to peck at scraps on the ground at the platform. They would chase away bigger birds such as plovers and guinea fowl that shrieked and chattered angrily as they flapped out of the way of ear-flapping elephants. Rundi was often satisfied with just chasing birds away by charging a few steps forwards, spreading her ears and sometimes letting out a little trumpet until the birds had retreated four or five metres. Muku on the other hand would bellow, run at them and chase them far across the grassland. He looked so much like a little cartoon drawing when he did this: tail out, ears spread, trumpeting squeakily, dust clouds rising up in his wake. When he was done Muku would wander back, swinging his head from side to side, swaying his trunk all over the place, eyes shining in excitement, or was it satisfaction? The guinea fowl obviously decided that half a tonne of elephant bearing down on them, trumpeting and ear flapping, wasn't a serious threat because they kept coming back to clean up scraps at the platform and the little chasing game could be seen almost every day.

It was a very different matter when it came to the eland. Standing two metres tall, a good half metre higher than the elephants, the eland with their heavy, spiralled horns, made formidable challengers. The two eland approached the platform one afternoon, the older one leading the way. They stopped a few metres away from the elephant's vegetable pile. Rundi and Muku both spread their ears, trumpeted and ran towards the eland. Casually, almost superciliously, the older of the two eland lowered his head, undoubtedly showing his horns to the elephants, and then slowly raised his head again, displaying his size advantage. This behaviour was something new to the elephants; everything else ran away from them. Muku immediately retreated from the eland, turned and ran in the opposite direction, bellowing and screaming as if the devil was on his heels. In fact Muku made such a noise that they could hear his trumpeting from the office, alerting Oscar to the fact that something unusual was going on.

"What's wrong?" Oscar asked, arriving at the platform slightly out of breath...

"Come and watch Oscar, the elephants and eland are having a showdown."

I pointed to Muku who was away in the distance, observing from afar, and we watched as Rundi stood still, facing down the eland. For long, agonising minutes Rundi didn't move and the eland didn't move; it was clear that neither were going to show a sign of weakness. Finally Rundi turned her back on the eland and walked back to the pile of vegetables where she ate a couple of leaves.

Rundi was obviously nervous of the eland and kept turning her head to look back and shaking her trunk violently from side to side. Rundi slowly made her way to the other side of the vegetable pile so she was facing the eland and carried on half heartedly picking up cabbage leaves and frequently shaking her head and trunk, snorting noisily. When the eland got brave and moved a couple of steps closer, Rundi reacted immediately with another charge.

Again the eland didn't move, just dropped his head slightly, showing off his big horns in threat and stood his ground, forcing Rundi to retreat again. Returning to the vegetable pile Rundi rumbled loudly and sniffed the air, perhaps looking for back up from Muku who was eating dry grass quite a distance away. Rundi gave one last charge at the eland, stopped short when it didn't move and then she gave up. She did it with style though, not running and squealing the way Muku had done but slowly, almost deliberately slowly, she gave up her claim to the vegetables. She almost sauntered off, making her way into the dry, unpalatable grass where Muku had been waiting watching all the time. You could almost see the droop of Rundi's shoulders and she half heartedly ate a few mouthfuls of dry grass, all the time looking across to the platform, watching as their prized vegetables were guzzled by the eland. The eland ate their fill of lettuce, tomatoes and cabbages, spending half an hour seeking out the greenest, most succulent leaves and fruits.

"Shouldn't we chase them away?" Oscar asked.

"Let's wait a bit Oscar. It would be better if the elephants chased them away."

Like waiting for a child in the playground to stand up to a bully, Oscar and I stood on the platform until the eland had eaten their fill and sauntered off. Round one was over and the score was eland one, elephants nil.

Having been victorious once, the pair of eland made it a regular occurrence to wander down to the platform and eat their fill of vegetables. Late every afternoon the routine was the same: the eland came, the elephants charged, Muku ran away, Rundi stood her ground but eventually retreated. I was adamant that we shouldn't interfere, there'd be no humans to help them if they were in the wild and the elephants were now certainly big enough to stand up for themselves. Things got out of hand when one afternoon the bellows and trumpet squealing from the platform, carried on the cold winter wind, seemed to fill the office. Oscar and I hurried down to the platform, walking faster and faster as the noise continued. We arrived to see Rundi having a show down with the eland. Literally head to head, with Rundi trumpeting and growling, the two animals pushed and shoved at each other. Muku, a safe distance away, ran backwards and forwards, trumpeting and defecating.

At last I couldn't watch anymore and went in to try and stop the war when the eland's horn was coming dangerously close to Rundi's eye.

"It's enough Oscar! Come, we've got to go and stop this."

Oscar and I went down the hill from the platform to the gate, unlocked it and rattled the chain, talking loudly in the hope that the eland would run away. There was no chance of that! The eland showed no fear of man or elephant, didn't run away as we approached and didn't even respond when we shouted and clapped our hands. Picking up lumps of hard dry soil, Oscar and I threw these at the eland to try and get him to back down but it was Rundi who ended the showdown herself.

Rundi just suddenly moved away from the eland, turned her back on him and casually wandered over to me, lifting my hand into her mouth and started sucking. Now Muku joined in and with a show of bravado came running over in full charge mode, trumpeting and raising dust, forcing the eland to retreat.

The events of that afternoon and the physical head to head shoving between Rundi and the eland had given me a fright. An elephant speared in the eye by and eland horn was not something I wanted to even think about; I knew I had to intervene. I changed the feeding time of the elephants, putting their vegetables out at different times and in different places in order to break what had become a frightening routine that could have easily escalated into something worse.

A few days later the shoe was on the other foot as I tried to chase the elephants away from someone else's food. For a long time we had been trying to encourage waterfowl to reside and nest at the pan in front of the platform. Every afternoon I put handfuls of coarse grain out on the ground a metre or so from the water's edge, hoping to catch the eyes of ducks flying home to roost and every morning the food was gone but there wasn't a duck to be seen. One night when out in the park trying to catch a poacher who had been laying snares on game trails in the heavily wooded area, I found out what was happening to the ducks' food. It was a bitterly cold night, moonless, still and very quiet. Dressed in jackets, gloves, balaclavas and boots we scanned the inky landscape. A crunch was heard and a shaded torch beam picked up Rundi and Muku carefully scooping up all the duck food with the tips of their trunks and ever so gently tipping it into their mouths. The culprits were caught red handed, or red nosed in this case!

Winter slipped away and the days grew longer and warmer but the food crisis wasn't over until the rains came and the grass started growing again. Every afternoon wheelbarrows were used to carry bags of food, sacks of vegetables and buckets of cubes and Simon and Joçam's arms got longer from the weight of carrying heavy watering cans full of molasses. Rundi and Muku soon figured out the afternoon routine. The squeak of a wheelbarrow would signal a raised trunk sniffing the air followed by head shaking with noisy ear slapping and then a fast walk to help the workers. And what a help they were! The hardest part of putting out the winter feed was keeping the elephants away from the molasses. I would measure the thick brown treacle into a watering can, dilute it with water and then a rose was fitted onto the can and the sticky mix was sprayed over the hay, lucerne and cotton seed making it more palatable and nutritious. When the sticky syrup was sprayed on the feed it lost a lot of its appeal for the elephants because then they had to eat the food in order to get the molasses. The real prize for them was to drink it neat, straight from the watering can and they did this at every opportunity. You had to really concentrate because if your attention was diverted, even for a few seconds, a trunk would silently drop down, dip into the can and suck out a third of the contents in a single go. I'd lost count of the number of times Simon and Joçam would trudge back to measure out more molasses because the elephants had drunk the first lot. Again the can would be filled and lugged back out into the game park, watched by two elephants who stood ever so innocently, side by side, with wet, sticky molasses tide marks on their trunks.

As the trees began to get their new leaves, signalling the start of spring and end of winter, the Woodlands was flooded with a riot of colour. It was nearly a year since the elephants had arrived at the Mukuvisi Woodlands and they often walked out on their own now, spending two or three hours at a time searching for desirable titbits in the light woodland. They would get to an area of favoured vegetation and stretch their trunks up to strip succulent new leaves from the ends of twigs. As lower leaves were cleared they pulled branches down to get to higher ones, much to the outrage of preservationists who shouted louder and louder to "control those damned elephants," instructing me to give them more vegetables. But they didn't want more vegetables; the elephants obviously wanted more natural food: "the kind that grows on trees," I told the voices of dissent; they wanted the silky soft, delicate new leaves on the trees. Rundi and Muku were barely eighteen months old and the damage they did to the trees at that age was seasonal; the instinctive response to a simple fact of life called spring. After four months of dry, tough grass the sudden miraculous appearance of green was irresistible and not only to elephants. Everywhere I looked, animals were eating new leaves, and not just browsers but the grazers too. Impalas stood on anthills and chomped a distinct browse line on trees, wildebeest and zebra beheaded every new shrub within days of its appearance; eland and elephants worked tirelessly on the higher leaves: elephant pulling branches down with their trunks, eland twisting them off with their horns. As the days passed and the vegetation got denser with new leaf, the damage became less noticeable and the critics grew quiet again. Even the rubbing posts disappeared as leaf laden branches hung down and concealed the evidence.

Scattered throughout the woodland were trees which were used as rubbing posts by the animals. Why one particular tree should be chosen and used again and again as a rubbing post was a mystery but it was definitely the case. I often watched the elephants stop at a tree and then spend as long as fifteen minutes there, taking it in turns to rub backwards and forwards against the tree. After a while the bark got distinctively smoother as rough pieces wore off until it became a highly polished smooth patch on the tree. While one elephant rocked slowly back and forth relieving an itch or massaging a particular spot on its side, neck or backside, the other elephant would stand patiently nearby, waiting its turn. The harsh rasping noise of skin against bark could be heard over the sound of birds and it was hard not to stop and watch at what was the elephants' obvious delight: head down, trunk floppy and even eyes closed. The elephants always waited for each other while the rubbing post ritual went on and it was only when both had had their turn and were satisfied that they would quietly head off into the trees to continue browsing. I began to feel that Rundi and Muku seemed at last to have settled down, calmed down and become comfortable in their adopted environment.

TEN

....

When Roaland Jooste, parasitologist at the Government Veterinary Department phoned one morning to say he had found ten million coccidian eggs in one gram of faeces in the latest batch of dung samples from the elephants, I knew that we had an enormous problem. In fact I thought there was a very real chance we might even lose the elephants. When I had started collecting dung samples for the Government Veterinary Department I wasn't very knowledgeable about most parasites. Like most Zimbabweans who had grown up in a mixture of urban and country areas I knew about the more visible, sensational parasites. Things like ring worms which formed little white circles under your skin which often scarred you for the rest of your life. I knew about putzi flies that laid their eggs in damp clothes on the washing line and these then hatched into fat maggots under your skin; the writhing, squirming creatures had to be levered out with a sharp needle whose tip had been burnt in a candle to be sterilized! I knew about ticks which sat in the soft places on you, like in your groin, armpits or behind your knees where they feasted on your blood leaving the most unbearable itch and stinking headache when they'd gone. The parasites I had to deal with at the Mukuvisi Woodlands were entirely a different matter: invisible, silent killers.

Pulling out my file with all the results of the weekly faeces samples I paged through the results. Coccidia were regularly found in the elephant faeces but egg counts ranged from fifty to six hundred eggs per gram of faeces. Ten million eggs was a crisis to say the least! I immediately went to the game viewing platform dreading what I was sure I was going to find. Instead of seeing a debilitated, sick and weak pair of elephants, to my amazement and huge relief, Rundi and Muku looked absolutely fine. As I stroked and inspected them closely they went through the normal 'Good Morning' routine: sucking hands, sniffing and rumbling with a bit of good natured pushing and shoving thrown in for good measure. Roaland had told me that Coccidiosis was particularly prevalent in the warm season and attacks young animals. Symptoms of an infestation include diarrhoea, bleeding anal discharge, severe loss of weight and a high temperature. I watched as both Rundi and Muku urinated and defecated and everything looked normal with no sign of diarrhoea, blood or any other symptoms.

Returning to the office I phoned the veterinary department immediately. Roaland assured me that he had re-checked the samples twice and found the same result: an excessively high Coccidia count which should mean that I had a very sick elephant on my hands.

"I've just been with the elephants Roaland and they look absolutely fine. There's nothing unusual to see, urine and dung look normal, there's no diarrhoea or blood or anything of concern."

"OK let's just keep a close watch on this. Can we have a faeces sample from the elephants every day until we get to the bottom of this?"

Roaland explained that coccidian cysts are found in warm, wet bedding and so I did a major blitz on the elephants stable under the platform. It resembled a typical messy teenager's bedroom and Simon and I embarked on a cleanup. We pulled out all the bedding straw and even though I knew the parasites were miniscule and invisible to the naked eye, I found myself continually looking for writhing, squirming worms or fat little maggots but instead only found half chewed sticks, bits of crackly dry cabbage and a strange number of ostrich feathers. Everything went onto a giant bonfire. The floor and walls of the stable were scrubbed with disinfectant and when it was dry a giant new elephant size bed of thick, deep straw was laid out in their stable.

The next morning Roaland phoned with the results of the latest samples. He had found nothing, no coccidian at all. It was all a mystery, Roland was convinced that his initial findings had been correct but in the week that followed we took samples every day and there was no sign of coccidia at all: it had disappeared. Or that's what I thought.

With the massive coccidian oocyst count still on my mind, I started doing my daily patrols very early in the morning to reassure myself that the elephants were fine.

"Aah but you are too early today," Oscar mumbled just after six in the morning, rubbing sleep out of his eyes as he unlocked the padlock on the gate at the main road. This was long before the time of cell phones so I'd had to wake Oscar quarter of an hour before by calling him on the office phone when I was leaving home. The office phone was hooked up to a loud siren mounted on the wall outside Oscar's house so there was no chance of sleeping through it.

"Sorry Oscar, I want to walk early so I can make sure the elephants are OK."

"Mr Roaland must have made a mistake," Oscar muttered, shaking his head and yawning, waiting for me to set off so he could go back to his warm bed.

Letting myself in at the game gate there was no sign of the elephants so I assumed they'd already gone walking and I wandered down the path towards the small dam to check on the state of the mud and see if they were there. It was a very still and quiet morning broken only by a few birds' calls and I looked up to see a perfect V formation of ducks flying overhead. Even though it was autumn it was still very cold in the early mornings and my breath left a puff of white mist rising up in my wake. The dew was thick on the grass with beads of moisture hanging swollen and glistening on the tips of the tall dry grass. Having had more than a few frightening incidents with snakes, I had a bad habit of looking at the ground when I walked so I didn't see the elephants until I was almost at their side. It never failed to surprise me how two giant creatures could keep so still and be so quiet. Immediately two trunks went up to sniff me and they rumbled their greeting. They were standing side by side and as I put my hand out to stroke Rundi, Muku immediately started sucking her ear. Still trying to break him of this bad habit, I stepped forward and pushed him off Rundi's ear and at that moment saw that they were not alone.

Standing between the two elephants was a large, hairy bushpig. The menacing looking creature seemed as surprised as I was at this very unexpected meeting. His wiry hair rose up along his back making him look even bigger and me feel even more alarmed. I had no idea of the temperament of the bushpig or what I should do but soon found out. With his hair still standing up the bushpig put its head down and charged straight at me, answering both of my questions to which there was only one answer: run!

Heart pounding I ran, stumbling over big clumps of wet grass trying to find the easiest, straightest route to the fence. Luckily it wasn't far away and reaching for a hand hold I climbed up the mesh as fast as I could, only stopping when I got to the barbed wire strands at the top. Twisting round I looked down and saw the pig standing directly beneath me. The bushpig gave a throaty snort, scratched at the ground and sniffed the fence. I could have sworn that was his bad breath I smelt, drifting up in the mist cloud of his exhalations! The pain and throbbing in my fingers from hanging onto the diamond mesh fence was excruciating and I had a sudden and unexpected need to go to the loo when I thought about the rusting lower strands of the fence, hoping they wouldn't give out on me. I stayed still, waiting for the bushpig to go away. After a few more scratches at the ground and mucus-dripping sniffs at the wire, the bushpig turned around and trotted back into the long dry grass, invisible in seconds. I stayed where I was, hanging onto the wire until I thought my fingers would drop off and then the elephants arrived. Rundi lifted her trunk and sniffed at my trousers above her while Muku began a minute inspection of the soles of my shoes. The elephant with the shoe fetish was at it again, I thought, the notion dissolving my fear and the stress of the past few minutes. Finally I decided that it was safe and the bushpig wasn't coming back so I climbed down from the fence, took a wide detour around the dam and carried on with my patrol, followed by two happy, healthy elephants. It was a long time before I could get the image of the bushpig charging at me out of my head and even longer before I stopped questioning the peculiar friendship between a bushpig and two elephants.

All the workers thought my encounter with the pig and fence climbing abilities were extremely funny and I caught them sniggering, snorting and chuckling every time they saw me for the next few days. I felt a little ashamed of myself but knew that I would do exactly the same thing if a similar occasion arose. Within days of my meeting with 'Porky,' as I had nick-named the bushpig, the workers also had a couple of surprise meetings in store for them.

Simon's first task of the day was to clean out the elephants' stable under the platform, remove the manure, take out any wet straw, rake around the doorway and puff up the bedding, adding more when necessary. Having done the job every morning for a long time, Simon had an efficient routine all worked out. He would feed the hosepipe through the wire fence, turn the tap on and then push his wheelbarrow, which held a pitch fork and shovel, through the gate and straight to the elephants' stable, picking up the hosepipe on the way. On the day that Simon met the bushpig the routine was the same as always until he went in the doorway of the stable and there, asleep on the scattered straw were two elephants and their friend the bushpig, all fast asleep. Astounded by the sight, Simon let go his hold on the wheelbarrow and as the tools clattered to the ground, the bushpig awoke and tore straight at him. Just as I had done a few days earlier, Simon also didn't wait around when confronted by a charging, bristly, angry pig. He scaled the game fence, much to the delight of thirty school children who had just arrived at the platform and witnessed the whole thing from above. Although shaken by the encounter, Simon was very proud of his fence climbing skills and I felt a little less silly; Simon and I were now partners in escape techniques!

I was intrigued as to how the bushpig had got into the game park in the first place and it was Oscar who gave me the background.

"This big murungu (white man) came one day and in the back of the car he had a box and I knew something was inside because it kept jumping around."

"Moving around," I corrected him.

"No, jumping around! Whatever was inside was very cross and the box was jumping around all over the back of the car."

"My goodness! What happened then?"

"Well, I called Raymond and we thought maybe he had a baby or something in there because it was screaming. Really screaming like a child!"

"And then?"

"The man said he wanted to put the box into the game area. It's a pig, he told me! Straight away I said "No!" we don't allow pigs at Mukuvisi."

Oscar's face creased with smiles at the memory of the incident. He chuckled while he rolled and lit his home made cigarette, a master at the art of storytelling! "He said I must phone for the Manager, but I refused. I just told him, we aren't allowed to have pigs here."

"That's right," I said nodding, totally captivated by the story, waiting for Oscar to continue.

"Well then he got really cheeky, you know, shouting at me and Ray, saying we are stupid. That was a bad thing for him to say to us. He wasn't a good man. He got in the car and drove away from here, very fast."

"What happened next?" I asked.

"You know, in those days, I was just a worker like the others, not the Foreman," Oscar said, proudly straightening up and caressing the collar of the much coveted, beige uniform that indicated his present status. "I was doing my patrol of the fence one day and I found an empty box lying near the wire of the fence, down there by the bridge and I bent down to see if there was something inside, but there was nothing. The box was empty but then I looked at the wire and there was a hole cut in the fence. All around the hole I saw these hairs, brown hairs, hard hairs, harder than from a dog."

Oscar paused, frowning as he must have done when he knelt to inspect the hairs on the wire. "All around, inside the game fence, I could see something had been digging, everywhere there were holes in the sand, all over the place." He scratched his head and went on: "But they were not the holes that the guinea fowl make, these were deep holes and sand spread out all around. Then when I came back from checking the wire, I went inside the game area to fix the fence at the place where it had been cut and where something had been digging so many holes. I was surprised when I saw this animal running in the long grass. It was a pig, the pig from the man in the car."

"You mean he had cut a hole in the fence and just pushed it in?" I exclaimed.

"Sure! He must have done that because we never had a pig here before and then the man comes with the jumping box, and only a few days later, the bushpig is here."

Of course, there was no proof of Oscar's suspicions, but the denial of the request and Oscar's first sighting of a bushpig in the game park were remarkably close together and more than a little coincidental. It was impossible to work out how long ago that had been but after our second surprise meeting with the bushpig, I became a little concerned about the peculiar association between the elephants and the bushpig, and also worried that someone may get hurt. There were also serious veterinary concerns because bushpig and warthogs are both carriers of African Swine Fever, a disease which can be transmitted to domestic pigs resulting in major health problems and quarantine regulations. We hadn't introduced the bushpig into the game area and for now the best we could hope for was that it would leave of its own accord: not a difficult undertaking with our rusting game fence which was in dire need of repair.

The next encounter with the now infamous Porky again occurred early in the morning but this time it was Joçam's turn. Joçam had set out on a fence patrol on the outside of the game fence and was in a particularly sleepy state. Joçam couldn't walk very fast, something Oscar blamed on the fact that Joçam always wore other people's cast-off shoes which never fitted him and made locomotion fairly difficult, not to mention uncomfortable. Joçam always patrolled with a vicious panga which he almost dragged along the ground as he plodded along staring at his feet. Not far from the gate at the platform, Joçam virtually walked right into the bushpig, not seeing it until the very last moment. One version of the story was that not having the energy to scale the fence, Joçam had just turned around and shuffled away in his outsize shoes, closely followed by an angry bushpig which had broken out of the fence and was trying to find its way back in. Joçam later told us that he had turned back and chased the bushpig angrily with his panga. I was never sure which version to believe because by then everyone was desperate to be able to report something a little more courageous than running away and climbing fences! As the days passed there were no more face to face encounters with the bushpig but evidence in the form of spoor and droppings at the platform, showed that not only had Porky found his way back into the game park, but had also renewed his association with the elephants: sharing their bedroom at night and leaving early in the morning before any of us arrived. I was still left with the lingering question about the ten million coccidian eggs. Had some pig's dung got mixed in with elephants' sample? I thought it might have and that's where all the parasites were but Roaland doubted it. Later he wrote:

"Elephant fecal matter is quite distinct from bush pig, the former being a lot coarser and the aroma somewhat more pleasing to the proboscis. We usually discarded the outer layer of faeces samples to eliminate contamination."

Whatever the scientific evidence, or the aroma levels, neither the elephants nor their strange bedfellow in the form of a fat angry, bushpig showed any signs of being sick, weak or debilitated and the parasite count disappeared as mysteriously as it had arrived. Then the bushpig disappeared too and when there had been no sightings or footprints in the game area or droppings in the elephants' bedroom for a couple of weeks, we made another concerted effort at patching up holes in the game fence: a never ending job.

Having just got over one strange animal relationship another possible encounter cropped up shortly afterwards but luckily it was a near miss and not nearly as difficult to cope with. It came in the form of an animal request, something we had on an almost weekly basis. A polite and well spoken man phoned me at home one afternoon and begged me to give homes to two wild hares that he had been looking after. At first I was suspicious as it was unusual for anyone to have hares in captivity, but the man was adamant that they were indeed what he said they were: wild hares that fended for themselves in an overgrown part of his garden. The man pleaded with me and at last I relented, phoned Oscar and said the hares could be released straight into the game park when they arrived. Thinking the matter was over, I forgot about the hares until Oscar phoned me at six in the evening.

"Can you come to the Woodlands?" Oscar asked.

"What's the problem Oscar, it's almost dark and I'm in the middle of cooking. Can't it wait till the morning?"

"Please come now!" he urged "I'm worried that Rundi and Mukuvisi are going to kill the rabbits."

"Kill the rabbits?" I echoed. Then I remembered the hares.

"OK, I'll be there in ten minutes." I couldn't quite understand why Rundi and Muku would be trying to kill two hares and should have been suspicious when Oscar said 'rabbits' but thought it was just a language difference. Leaning my bicycle on the step outside my office I trudged down to the game park in the deepening twilight; I found Oscar at the gate.

"What is it Oscar?"

He didn't answer, just shook his grey head slowly and pointed to the two supposedly wild hares. One beautifully soft, grey and white rabbit and one fluffy black rabbit, sat shivering by the gate in the game park. Cursing under my breath, I beckoned to Oscar and we went in and picked up the fluffy creatures before they fell victim to snakes, eagles and elephant's feet. Oscar said that the man arrived with the creatures in a cardboard box which he had placed in the game park, as per my instructions, with Oscar nearby to supervise. When the animals didn't race out of the box, Oscar decided to leave them alone thinking that they were just scared and would come out when they were ready. Going back to lock up that evening, Oscar discovered the bunnies who had emerged from the box and sat shivering and trembling, waiting to be rescued. Of course the donor hadn't left his name or contact details so I didn't get a chance to query his knowledge of the rabbit family and spent some time finding a suitable home for the pair the next day. I didn't dare even think what might have happened if Rundi and Muku had met the rabbits. Knowing Muku's fascination with carrying around all things soft, fluffy and feathery I knew it wouldn't have ended well.

ELEVEN

....

Heading out on an early patrol I started at the small pan in front of the game viewing platform which was finally bone dry. This was usually the moment we dreaded but the drought of 1986/87 gave us the opportunity we'd been waiting for. It had been decided that this would be an ideal time to deepen the shallow dam on the Chiraura River that we called the pan. Rolf Chenaux-Repond, the Manager of Highway Construction Company and one of the founder members of the Mukuvisi Woodland Association, had built the lower dam in 1982 and a year later constructed the pan in front of the game viewing platform, both free of charge. He now offered to carry out the much needed deepening of the pan on the same basis. Rolf was a long standing friend of the Mukuvisi and was always a pleasure to work with: polite, courteous and helpful. Over the years Rolf had spent much time in the Woodlands, observing and recording its birdlife, and later he assisted in compiling a checklist of the birds, thus adding to the educational information we had on the diversity of species around us.

After winter, as day time temperatures rose, the water level in the pan had gone down quickly. First we could see the bottom and then it began to emerge into the daylight, the clay shrinking and leaving big squares of baked mud. While the water level had been dropping the elephants had a ball. Mud baths were a daily routine and all they had to do was stagger out of their giant hay bed in the morning, shuffle across to the pan and flop down into the mud. Every day Rundi and Muku spent hours lying in the cool mud, squirting themselves and each other, rolling and cavorting to their hearts content.

Rolf had been monitoring the progress of the drying pan, waiting for the right time to commence work under optimal conditions. It was hard to believe how much silt had been washed into the pan in the four years since it was built, a process which had significantly reduced its storage capacity. The first part of the operation started with Rolf surveying the depth of the clay base of the pan; it was this clay which held the water and if it was insufficient it would have been necessary to line the pan with other impervious material brought on to the site, or to use an expensive membrane. First five test holes were dug, each a metre square and two metres deep. Once again I called on Joçam to do the job which he managed to complete in a very short time, even with continual interference from the elephants. We were delighted to hear that the natural clay extended more than two metres below the bottom of the pan. Luckily for me Rolf had a good sense of humour as when he came to do the survey work at the pan, Rundi and Muku had taken a liking to his tripod, removing and eating the leather straps!

The ground had to be rock hard before work could begin because heavy earthmoving plant was to be used for the job. By September conditions were suitable for the machines to move in. One Monday morning two very large, yellow items of earthmoving equipment, a bulldozer and a self- propelled scraper, appeared on site on low-bed trailers, along with two men and two drums of diesel fuel. The elephants took off, their wobbling grey backsides rapidly disappearing into the distance. The huge machine got to work excavating, scraping and heaping soil; the accompanying noise was deafening. Accustomed to the sound of birds and wind, the occasional braying of zebra and snorting of wildebeest, the assault on the senses of the two little elephants was immense. The relentless roaring of the huge 200 plus horsepower engines was too much for them, more so as the engines were left running when the operators needed a break or a drink and so kept growling on and on. Music, perhaps, to the ears of an earthmoving contractor but not to the animals.

I scanned the grassy vlei for signs of the elephants, the air shimmering with a mirage of heat haze and dust, finally spotting them in some thick grass near the lower dam. The elephants' routine had been drastically changed by the noisy activity at the pan. They could no longer just stroll fifty metres from the platform to have a drink or roll in the mud; now they had to walk a few hundred metres downstream along the Chiraura River to the small dam there. This was a bird watchers paradise where not so long ago Rundi had got stuck in the mud and now the only source of water in the game park area. The lower dam became a very busy place as all the animals had to go there to drink and for the elephants it also became a good hiding place when the big machines arrived.

"There's nothing to see today," we kept telling visitors as we turned them away when they arrived at the office.

A father and his two young sons arrived and I repeated the line.

"Sorry, we're bulldozing the pan and it's scared all the animals away."

"We don't mind!" said a little voice and I looked down to see two little faces glowing with excitement.

"We saw the bulldozer from the road, that's why we're here," Dad said. The little boys looked anxiously at me.

"You're welcome!" I said, "No charge today."

While the Dad stopped to get coffee at the kiosk the boys raced ahead. Watching a bulldozer was infinitely more exciting than watching sleeping animals.

Mid morning I went down to see how work was progressing and found Simon standing forlornly, two buckets of milk in his hands, waiting at the gate. The milk had a fine layer of dust on it and Simon too was getting a fine layer of dust all over him.

"No elephants," he announced mournfully. Rundi and Muku were still hiding down at the lower dam and when I said he'd have to take the milk and porridge to them because there was no way they were coming here, Simon's face grew even longer. It was a long walk and the buckets, two thirds full, were heavy. Joçam was passing and was recruited to help and I watched from the platform as the two men trudged off into the hanging dust to give the elephants their breakfast. When they were about half way to the dam Simon must have called the elephants because I saw two trunks appear above the grass and then two elephants emerged, running towards Simon and Joçam and the precious buckets of milk and porridge. Watching through binoculars I saw men meeting elephants, buckets being put down on the ground and trunks being dipped in. It just took a couple of minutes for the elephants to drain their buckets these days and when they were done they started following Simon and Joçam back towards the platform, changing their minds as soon as they saw the bulldozer and turning back to the dam.

At lunch time a blissful quiet fell over the Woodlands. The bulldozer needed refuelling and the men needed lunch. The choking pall of dust gradually settled but there wasn't an animal in sight. As soon as the dozer operators had gone out of the gate I went in search of the elephants. They hadn't had their usual morning ration of cubes or vegetables and there wasn't much goodness left in the dry brown grass. Rundi and Muku were still at the dam and followed me back without any hesitation. The noise and dust had gone and the bulldozer was now barely visible, parked at the bottom of the ever deepening pan. I led the elephants straight to their food and they wasted no time stuffing vegetables into their mouths making short work of broccoli, cabbage, tomatoes and carrots. I tipped a bucket of cubes onto the ground and these were also dispatched very rapidly. With the business of eating dispensed with, Rundi went to investigate the monster at the pan, followed cautiously by Muku. Even though he was bigger than her, he was still very much a baby when it came to mechanical monsters.

First they went to the dam wall where the excavated silt had been piled into big mounds. Rundi sniffed the drums of fuel, sucking the smell into her nose and then lifting her trunk and blowing the smell into her mouth, as if tasting it. She spread her ears and rumbled loudly and moved to the mounds of soft silt. Muku followed her and the pair stood head to head, smelling and rumbling until Muku obviously couldn't resist and lifted one foot onto a mound of soft sandy silt. He dropped onto his front knees, backside to the sky and pushed his forehead into the sand, rubbing his head from side to side, soon flattening the mound. He moved to the next pile and did the same there and before long Rundi joined in. Soon the elephants were causing chaos all along the pan wall. All the mounds of silt were flattened and reshaped, scattered and used as dusting powder, thrown over heads and backs with complete abandon and obvious delight.

At the end of the earth wall the elephants followed the gradual slope until they got to the deepest point and there came face to face with the monster bulldozer. Rundi's ears spread immediately and she reversed, obviously not having seen the machine until she was almost on top of it. Muku stood a little distance away, leant his head forward and stretched his trunk towards the scraper. The tip of his trunk not quite touching the enormous wheels, Muku sniffed deeply and then blew the smell into his mouth. At the taste of the smell he shook his head rapidly from side to side, ears slapping noisily against his back. Rundi put the tip of her trunk at the edge of Muku's mouth, smelling intently before she reversed again, ears spread out.

Muku's curiosity had been aroused and he took a very small step forward and again smelt deeply until he at last moved close enough to finally touch one of the huge tyres, the tip of his trunk carefully investigating the grooves in the tread. For a good ten minutes Muku thoroughly investigated the scraper's tyres, sniffing, touching, shaking his head and spraying an invisible smell into his mouth. Rundi wasn't interested in the machine at all; she explored the dam, scuffing loose soil, covering herself with dust and smelling everywhere. Hearing a whistle I looked up and saw Simon and the machine operators standing at the gate of the game park, waiting to come back in. Leaving the elephants I went to the gate and asked Simon to get a bag of cubes and come in and lead the elephants away on a long afternoon walk. As soon as he was ready, Simon called to Rundi and Muku who followed him immediately and when they were a distance away the bulldozer roared back into life and peace was shattered.

It took three days to complete the deepening of the pan and on the last morning, when the machines were parked ready for departure, their engines silent, we managed, at the request of the machine operators, to lure Rundi and Muku to the platform to have their milk. The men were delighted as we called them to stand close to the elephants and witness the speed drinking of milk and porridge. When the buckets were empty the men nervously stretched out their hands and touched the elephants, exclaiming at their tough, rough skin, shaking their heads in amazement and smiling widely. Just as the elephants had cautiously, suspiciously explored the bulldozer, now the tables were turned as the men did the same to the animals; hesitantly, fearfully they met the giants of the animal world. What stories they would have to tell around the supper table tonight and for a long time to come; imagine a machine operator going home and saying casually: I stroked an elephant today! When the men and their bulldozer had left, the pan looked enormous and was a metre and a half deeper than it had been, all it needed now was water. By the next day Rundi and Muku had reclaimed their territory and taken over the giant new sand pit. They spent hours scuffing, dusting, rolling and even sleeping in the oversize sand pit. I knew they had better make the most of it because within a few days I got the go ahead to pump water for an hour a day from the borehole into the pan: just to give enough for a little a puddle of water in the mornings for the elephants to drink from.

Normally we pumped water from the borehole to the pan every day during winter to maintain the water level but this year, because of the earth works, we hadn't pumped water for months so the five hundred metre pipe line and outlet into the pan needed to be checked. Oscar and I worked on this together. At first we couldn't find the pipe's outlet into the pan because it was covered with soil from the earthworks. We tracked along the pipe line markers and finally located the outlet, clearing sand out of it with a long rod. The pipe outlet was located about half way down the depth of the pan and we propped it up on blocks to stop it getting buried.

Oscar walked the five hundred metres back to the borehole shed which was outside the game area and back up the hill to start the engine while I stayed at the outlet pipe in the pan. By now Rundi and Muku had sauntered over to find out what was going on in their sand pit and the three of us stood looking at the ground. I knew what I was waiting for and they were just keeping me company. While Rundi and Muku scooped up little piles of sand and chucked it over their heads I squatted down waiting to hear the first gurgle of water coming down the line. When nothing happened I took the clearing rod and pushed it as far as it would go into the pipe. It met with some resistance but after some wiggling and pushing to loosen the block suddenly there was a gurgling noise and I knew it was near.

At the unexpected gurgling noise from underground, Rundi and Muku both turned and ran away, tails out, ears spread, high pitched trumpeting. With delight and great satisfaction I stood and watched as the water poured out of the pipe onto the soft, newly excavated soil. The first drops of water into our brand new pan, what a delight. I bent down, rinsed my hands and then cupped and lifted them to my mouth, tasting the first mouthful of cool, clear water to come into the new pan. As the earth around the outlet became saturated and the clay turned dark and then black, I looked at my watch to time one hour.

Before long Oscar arrived, accompanied by Simon, Ray and Joçam and we stood together, all smiling and chattering at this wondrous occasion. Water is never taken for granted in Africa and it was pure bliss to see it gushing out and soaking the ground. Like me, the men also crouched down, washed their hands and drank a mouthful of water. Finally, seeing all of us standing around in the pan laughing and chatting, Rundi and Muku wandered back. You could almost see the embarrassment on their faces as they trundled along, shaking their heads from side to side and flapping their ears. With delight we watched as Rundi's foot sunk into the newly wet ground. It seemed to take a moment for her to register that something was different; her trunk dropped down to smell the dampness and slowly a little puddle of water began to form around her toes and that was it: heaven had returned! As fast as the water pooled so the elephants sucked it up, mud and all and after an hour's pumping there was still only the smallest of puddles left in the bottom of a very big hole.

The following morning we ran the pump again. Rundi and Muku had been busy, there was no puddle left, only a big flattened area where they had been rolling and cavorting in the mud. The water ran through the pipe from the borehole a lot faster this time now that all the debris had been flushed out of the line and the puddle grew quickly. While Rundi sucked from the puddle, Muku wandered along the stream of water running down from the outlet. The water slowed and diverted around his feet before finding its way again, filling in his footsteps, re-routing a path to the puddle at the bottom. Then Muku discovered the outlet of the pipe and after carefully inspecting and sniffing it he tried to drink straight from the gushing pipe. What fun to watch! The tip of his trunk in the end of the pipe caused the water to squirt in all directions, including onto him, leaving dark blotches on his dry, dusty skin. Muku was hooked and for ten minutes didn't move, sucking cool clear water straight from the outlet. Eventually, thirst satisfied, he shook his head mightily, smelled the pipe once more and then went to lie in the pool that was again forming at the bottom of the Pan. Rundi was already there, stretched out on her side in the puddle, covered in mud.

It took quite a few days for the daily pumping to produce anything substantial at the bottom of the pan: earth and elephants greedily sucking it up almost as fast as we could pump it. Many days I cheated, and I suspect many nights Oscar cheated too, leaving the borehole running for much longer than the hour we'd been permitted. Slowly the puddle got bigger, the pool became a pond and then a waterhole, big enough for the other animals to come and drink from and so life returned to the Mukuvisi. Rolf had one more touch to add: he made a water level marker for the pan, painted and carefully numbered the metres and centimetres before planting it at the pan. The elephants showed their appreciation for this piece of scientific equipment by using it as a rubbing post, bending and re-shaping the marker to their liking!

As the days got longer and hotter and we waited for the rain to bring a change in scenery and diet, the next diversion for the elephants came from the matamba trees (*Strychnos spinosa*). All of the wild orange trees, or matambas as they were known locally, were covered with hard green fruits, the size and shape of cricket balls; dark green, gradually turning yellow and then a deep orange as they ripened. The elephants loved matambas; we had hand fed them with the fruit almost from their very first week at the Woodlands when they were still in the boma. In those days we had to crack them open for the elephants, smashing them on the ground to break the hard, woody shells but now the elephants picked the matambas for themselves and seemed to have located every tree in the game park. They started with ripe fruits that fell to the ground and then moved on to those still attached to the trees which were normally small in height making the fruit easy to get at. Sometimes we saw the elephants eating the matambas when they were still green but usually they left them lying on the ground, returning when they were ripe. Occasionally when I was out patrolling I would collect a few ripe matambas if I found them on the ground and bring them back for the elephants. I never bought more than a few at a time because they were cumbersome to carry and I knew that other animals in the game park also ate them.

Tipping the wild oranges out at the platform the hard balls would roll around and you had to get out of the way very quickly because the elephants pushed and shoved anything in the way as they rushed to grab the fruits. Picking the complete matamba up in a curled trunk they would plop the whole thing into their mouths, trails of silver dribble streaming, showing just how eager they were for this treat. Usually the matambas were eaten shell and all by the elephants, a noisy, complicated affair as the skin is extremely tough and hard. Other times, when the elephants weren't in such a frenzy, they would carefully put one foot on the matamba and exert just enough pressure to crack the shells and expose the juicy, smooth, light brown pulp which they scooped out with the tips of their trunks.

About fifty metres outside the main gate of the game park was a particularly fine matamba tree, its branches drooping heavily, crowded with fruits. The elephants weren't the only ones who loved matambas, all the workers liked them too. Everyone kept their eye on the tree outside the game gate; it was safe from animals there but as soon as the first hint of yellow appeared on a fruit it would disappear. Often Oscar and the others would argue over the matambas, accusing each other of taking more than their fair share. Oscar suggested that instead of anyone taking them home, all the ripening matambas should be left to ripen on the ground under the tree and at an agreed time everyone would sit together and have a feast.

It all sounded very democratic and sociable the only problem was that the elephants were also watching the matambas ripening on the ground, from the other side of the game gate. Often you would see them with their trunks raised in the direction of the matamba tree outside the gate; they must have been able to smell the heady, fermenting fruit as it ripened and eventually it drove them to desperate measures. Every time anyone went in the game gate they would be met and passed by two elephants going in the opposite direction.

You had to be very quick to close and padlock the gate before the elephants were upon you and if you weren't careful they were out. Rundi and Muku knew exactly where they were going and would run straight to the matamba tree: ears spread, trunks raised, saliva dripping from the edges of their mouths. You could almost see the defiance in their eyes, daring you to try and stop them. Arriving at the tree the pair immediately started to snatch up the ripening matambas and devour them: crack, crunch, swallow, repeat!

Getting the elephants to go back through the game gate wasn't easy once they had a taste for the matambas. After their second or third break out I insisted that no matamba fruits were to be left on the ground under the tree; they all had to be collected and thrown in to the elephants, except of course for a couple each for workers.

Once Rundi and Muku had learnt to rush at the game gate and escape to greener pastures, innocence was lost; after that it was never easy to go in and out of the game gate and we all had to be careful and alert. The diamond mesh on the gate became pushed in and permanently imprinted with the shape of their heads and most of us got into the habit of throwing a handful of cubes or vegetables over the fence to get the elephants away from the gate before daring to unclip the padlock.

In order to distract the elephants from their new escaping trick I was always on the lookout for things that kept them away from the game gate. The perfect opportunity arose one morning when I arrived to find a little plastic ice cream box on my desk.

"What's this?" I asked Mike Muvishi, the Education Officer, pointing to the tub balanced on top of a pile of papers.

"Worms I think," he answered, "Gary and Justin dropped them off."

Hearing the names Gary and Justin I knew there could be any number of scary things inside the box from spiders to rodents or worse. Opening the box very cautiously, I saw a writhing mass of black and yellow caterpillars swarming over one solitary leaf at the bottom of the container. The caterpillars were silk worms that we'd talked about and I was going to put them into the fish tank in the office, a tank which had long since ceased to function as an aquatic environment; its last occupants being baby tortoises and then a baby crocodile.

All the children who came to the Woodlands loved peering through the glass of the fish tank to see what unexpected creatures it contained and the silk worms didn't disappoint. Not having kept silk worms since I was a child, I'd forgotten how much they ate and soon realised it was going to be a mission keeping the worms satisfied. The nearest mulberry tree was about a kilometre away growing near a corner of the game fence so I asked Oscar to tell whoever was on fence patrol duty every morning to encourage the elephants to go with them and to stop and pick a bag of leaves on their way past the tree.

Joçam was on fence patrol that week and the following morning he stomped into the office and stood over me.

"Morning Joçam," I said without looking up, "everything OK on the fence?" This was the same thing I said to him every morning when he came back from fence patrol.

"I get them," he said.

That made me look up, who had he got, I wondered?

"It's the right ones?" he asked, holding out three single mulberry leaves which were supposed to be enough to feed about forty silk worms!

Smiling I took the three leaves from him. "Thanks Joçam , those are the right ones."

Oscar, who had come in to see what was going on asked me if everything was alright.

"Yes, thanks Oscar, but I think this won't quite be enough."

"Not enough?" he asked, "for worms?"

"Oscar, you see how many worms I've got in here? Let's just take out one worm and put it in this box with one leaf ok?"

Oscar nodded suspiciously.

"You watch that worm Oscar and see how long before the leaf is finished, then you'll see what I mean."

Not saying a word Oscar took the box over to the kiosk where he was working and I got back to my desk. Less than an hour later Oscar was back.

"It's hungry!" he announced plonking the box down.

Feigning innocence, I opened the box before looking up to meet Oscar's eyes and couldn't keep the smile away. The box contained one worm, no leaf and a lot of little black droppings. Oscar called Joçam and gave him a lengthy biology lesson on the eating habits of silk worms, the crux of it apparently being that I had forty silk worms and needed a lot more than three leaves!

The next day Joçam, never one for half measures, went from the sublime to the ridiculous. He came back from fence patrol with a 20 kg mealie meal sack jammed with mulberry leaves. Even squashing them down really tightly, the leaves didn't all fit into the large fish tank in the office. Joçam was so proud of himself that I hated having to hurt his feelings and thanked him graciously for carrying such an enormous bag of leaves back for my worms. The next day I gave Oscar a plastic shopping bag to give to Joçam, saying that I thought this would be plenty. As the days passed the silk worms gorged themselves until they reached massive proportions and then gradually began to spin silk around themselves and go into cocoons, undoubtedly exhausted from having had to eat so much of Joçam's bounty! Poor Joçam, now I had to tell him I didn't need any leaves at all but at least the elephants were getting a good long walk every day and had their minds taken off the oh so tempting matamba tree on the other side of the gate.

TWELVE

....

In November 1987 the drought broke and the long awaited rains arrived. Within ten days the Woodlands was transformed from dry brown to soggy green. After months of bright blue sky we looked with relief on heavy, dark skies filled with towering grey clouds. The rain brought everything to life: trees became green and glossy, their dusty coatings washed off in the rain; green grass sprouted everywhere; the river began to flow and the animals got ready for birthing season. Wildebeest ran in giddy circuits across the vlei, zebra cavorted and kicked and all the while the elephants just plodded along. It was surprising to watch Rundi and Muku in the rain because they never tried to take cover, even in the heaviest, pounding storms when the skies flashed with lightning and roared with thunder. The two elephants would stand, either side by side or head to head, ears forward, as the rain streamed over their bodies. Usually they let their trunks hang loosely to the ground with only the tip slightly curled up.

With renewed enthusiasm the elephants explored the vlei and woodland, finding delectable new treats everywhere. Their walking got slower as they feasted on soft sweet grass, plucking it from the ground, shaking the soil off and putting it in their mouths; uprooting the next clump while still chewing on the first. They drove me mad as I stooped to try and identify a flower or shrub but before I'd even managed to count leaves or petals a grey trunk would drop down and the specimen was gone, from nose to mouth in an instant. How did they know which plants to eat I wondered; was it the smell, texture or colour? Perhaps more to the point, how did they know which plants not to eat, which plants were poisonous? Somehow they did know the difference and I learnt that if I wanted to identify plants I had to walk without Rundi and Muku!

On many occasions I would get caught in a rain storm whilst out on patrol and as I tried to shelter under dense trees, Rundi and Muku would walk out into a clearing and stand in the rain, getting completely soaked. When the storm passed and I emerged relatively dry, they would lovingly dab their wet trunks on me or rub their wet sides up against me. Knowing their fear of trucks and machines I thought the rumbling and crashing of a thunder storm would terrify them but they took absolutely no notice. As the water level in the dams rose, the elephants' favourite rolling place became submerged but they soon established new ones and it was a huge relief not to have to worry about food and water for them and the other animals anymore.

Just before Christmas 1987, when Muku was 23 months old, his tusks erupted causing a great deal of excitement. Simon, who spent a lot of time with his hand in the elephants' mouths, was naturally the first to notice. He was so excited when he made the discovery that it took a while to understand what he was trying to say in his agitated babble.

"It's outside! Muku got tooth outside!" he kept repeating, grinning and pointing to his own cheek. The faster he talked the more obvious it became that this was something I needed to go and see straight away.

"Let's go," I said gesturing for Simon to lead the way.

Heading to the game viewing platform we stopped to get some cubes and then went straight down to see the elephants. Muku obligingly opened his mouth to receive the cubes and we both got a clear view of his newly erupted, small white tusks. Muku was completely unconcerned as we peered into his mouth and put our hands in to touch his new tusks: the first human hands on new born ivory; this was a landmark day. When Muku's trunk was down and his mouth closed, the tusks were not visible, the only sign that something was there were two small lumps on either side of his top lip and these were only noticeable if you were looking for them.

Simon and I were as excited as any parent at their child's first tooth and we couldn't wait to tell everyone the momentous news. Muku suddenly found himself the centre of attention with all the workers wanting to hand feed him and put their fingers in the sides of his mouth, to touch this new ivory for the first time. Rundi was completely left out of all the excitement, her tusks were not visible at all yet but we also gave her extra cubes and made a fuss of her so that jealousy wouldn't cause a problem between the two elephants.

The elephants tusk is the equivalent to an upper incisor and the tusk that we could see now was Muku's permanent tusk and would be present for the rest of his life. It would continue to grow throughout his life but also be gradually worn down at the tip by wear and usage. As delighted as I was at the visible emergence of Muku's tusks I knew that from that day on his life would be in danger from poachers. It wouldn't be long before Rundi began to get swellings on her upper lip and her tusks also emerged. The kids had come of age.

While everyone exclaimed about the elephant's new tusks and visitor numbers increased dramatically, the rain set in. The usually small, gently flowing Chiraura River which ran under the fence and across the west of the game park had turned into a raging torrent. A big problem started where the river ran under the game fence and flowed through three massive drain pipes. We had erected a swinging gate over the drains to allow debris through but prevent the entry of dogs and it was this gate which caused the problem. As the river rose and the water speed increased, it bought with it large amounts of stream-side litter in the form of bulrushes, rocks, grass and large tree branches. At the height of flow, a huge branch wedged the gates closed causing a great build up of litter against the drains. With no other possible route except upwards, the water rose higher and higher until it overtopped the bridge above the drains. Floating litter then met another barrier in the form of the game fence running across the top of the bridge. Joçam discovered the damage whilst on fence patrol and it took a bit of doing to understand what he was trying to tell us.

"Big tree," he said making a circle with his arms to indicate the girth of the obstacle.

"Very, very big! Full up water over here!" he continued and now pointed to a spot above his head. "All falling down, all out, everything out, running away."

Hard as I tried, I could not make sense of what Joçam was desperately trying to get me to understand so called for Oscar. After some minutes Oscar turned to me.

"We better go and see," he said.

"What is it, what's happened?"

"Maybe a tree has fallen on the fence, I don't know what he's trying to say."

"OK, let's just go and see. Where Joçam?"

Joçam didn't answer, but beamed, delighted that at last he had managed to get our attention to the disaster he had discovered. With Joçam leading, we set out to the river below the boma and were soon joined by all the other workers. Initially we were all speechless at the sight. Twenty or more metres of game fence had been dragged downstream. Steel poles, previously embedded in thick concrete, lay metres downstream as if plucked out of the earth by a great hand from above. Initial silence became gasps, exclamations, laughter and finally, excited chatter. Stripping off my gum boots I gingerly stepped onto the bridge into water which was above my knees.

"No," shouted Oscar, "come back, you will be drowned, come back!"

I ignored him, someone had to see what was blocking the gate and drains and I was the best swimmer of all of us. Hanging on to one strand of wire that had managed to get tangled into the bridge sides, I made my way to the middle of the bridge. The pull of the water was strong against my legs and the water was very abrasive as it was filled with litter. I could see the branch jamming the gate and bent to try and shift it with one hand, the water immediately covering my waist and pulling at my arms. The current was really fierce and with only one hand free, I knew that I didn't have the strength. Straightening up and now almost completely soaked, I turned and shouted to Oscar.

"I need help, the water is too strong. Can you come out and help me?"

"Come back," he shouted over the noise of the torrent, "come back!"

Returning across the bridge I made it to the safety of the shore and explained the whole problem to the others.

"We must wait until the water goes down," Oscar said immediately.

"No, we can't wait Oscar, it may take hours for the river to go down and by then the drains might also get pulled out of the river. We have got to move that log now, we don't want to lose the drains, or even the bridge."

Then followed a lengthy argument in Shona between all the workers and after some minutes I interrupted.

"We're wasting time! The sooner we get the branch through the gates, the sooner the water will go down. There's lots to do, the fence has to be repaired, poles put back in, wire re-attached. Come on! Who's going to come and help me?"

In his usual inimitable way, Oscar had made a decision before I'd even finished speaking. Ordering Simon and Joçam to roll up the legs of their overalls and remove their boots, he instructed them to get the log out of the swinging gate above the drain pipes. This was no doubt one of the advantages of being the Foreman! I knew that Oscar was scared of water so I didn't challenge his decision and I led the pair out onto the bridge. Whenever I could I tried to join in on the jobs; that was how I was able to gauge what was and wasn't possible and more importantly it made me one of the team.

Arriving at the middle of the bridge Joçam, who could not swim, plunged both of his arms under the water. Not holding onto anything, the pull of the water immediately took him under.

"Simon, grab him!" I screamed and we both put an arm down and wrenched a spluttering, choking Joçam to the surface.

"Are you alright Joçam?" I asked.

Scraping the water off his face, Joçam grinned and Simon and I burst out laughing. What was Joçam thinking I wondered? A question it would be pointless to ask! Now, instead of being wet up to our knees we were all soaked through.

"Right, now look, hold on with one hand," I said demonstrating and both men grinned. All three of us grasped the one tangled wire, bent over and each grabbed the branch, managing to straighten it and slide it through the swinging gate. Almost immediately the speed of the water going under the bridge increased dramatically, bringing with it another great mat of reeds, sticks, plastic bottles and other litter which formed a barrier against the gate and slowed the water again.

"I can help," a voice shouted in my ear, startling me so badly that I nearly lost my grip and went overboard!

It was Leonard, he hated to miss out on anything and by then I was delighted to step aside and let someone else take over. Leaving Simon, Joçam and Leonard standing knee deep in water on the bridge manoeuvring obstacles and clearing the swinging gate, I went back to the bank to join Oscar.

Oscar and Everisto had begun salvaging what they could of the fence wire and steel poles so I sloshed back through centimetres of water that had accumulated on the path after days of rain and went off to get changed. So used to getting soaked in the rain almost every day, I had taken to keeping a change of clothes in the office.

Later I went back to see how the repair work was getting on, taking a slow meander along the river bank. The river looked to be almost two metres higher than normal and well over its banks, the grass flattened and strewn with flood litter. Crabs caught in the rising water were stranded on firm ground and rushed around with outstretched pincers, clearly disorientated, trying to find somewhere secluded to hide and wait for the water to subside. At the pan the water was only a few centimetres from topping the wall, while the spillway was struggling to remove the flood waters fast enough. Dense stands of bulrushes along the river banks had completely disappeared along with the many dozens of weaver and bishop birds' nests they had supported. I stood staring at this devastation; it was a completely new landscape and a dramatic example of the force of nature. Heading back towards the bridge on the river I was soon met by the two elephants. Rundi and Muku walked with me all the way to the bridge and then we had great fun giving Muku branches to move that were obstructing the fence repairs. I don't know who was more delighted: man or elephant! It wasn't a very effective operation because Muku would lift a branch, wander off with it and then just abandon it, giving us more work clearing up afterwards. Standing with one hand on each elephant watching the men at work, I thought about what a struggle it had been rearing these two elephants and how gentle, loving and trusting they had become. It was hard to believe that they had been at the Woodlands for sixteen months already; despite all the dramas and problems the days had just flown past. In my heart I knew that the time was rapidly approaching when they would have to move on; soon they would be too big to say at the Mukuvisi Woodlands.

My niggling thoughts about the elephants outgrowing the Woodlands were reinforced when we had another escape. A big lunch function had been planned and everyone was busy preparing for the event. My 'to do' list was as long as my arm and was interrupted when a fancy car drove in the gate revealing Bill Gordon. Bill was a great friend and supporter of the Woodlands generating interest and donations all the time. The last time I'd seen Bill I promised to show him around the game park whenever it suited him and he had chosen today! He couldn't have chosen a worse time and to exacerbate things had bought some overseas guests with him. Not wanting to be rude I explained that we had a big function planned for later in the day and we agreed that just a visit to the elephants would suffice. At that moment a mini-bus drove in loaded with pre-school children who had also come to see the elephants. With my head whirling I foolishly decided to kill two birds with one stone.

"Let's all go and see the elephants together," I declared.

Bill and his guests smiled and nodded, the children chorused their delight and off we went. Twenty pre-school children scampered ahead of us along the path to the game viewing platform. Like frenzied wind-up toys the children zoomed around, detouring to tortoises, terrapins and crocodiles while we sauntered along behind. I knew that the children couldn't go any further than the game viewing platform and once they got there all sorts of things would keep them amused until we arrived: bones, skulls, feathers, specimens in bottles and beautiful murals on the walls.

Arriving at the platform with Bill and his guests I didn't realise that the elephants hadn't had their morning milk yet. Milk and porridge was still the highlight of their day and they always waited anxiously and impatiently for their buckets. When I didn't see Simon anywhere

I assumed the elephants had already had their milk so I unclipped the padlock and we all filed in through the gate. I was at the front, the children behind me, their teachers and Bill's guests followed and Bill took up the rear. It took only a few seconds for me to realise I had a problem. Suddenly Rundi started to run rapidly towards us and the open gate. It never failed to amaze me how fast these huge creatures could move but this wasn't the time to be marvelling at Rundi's agility and running skills.

"Hurry Bill, close the gate!" I shouted.

It was too late! Children scattered in all directions as the elephant charged towards the open gate. A split second too late Bill tried to close the gate on 500 kg of elephant. Impeccably dressed in a navy blazer and white trousers, Bill fell headlong into the mud while Rundi rushed past him, out of the gate and ran off in the direction of the car park.

The children were in a state; they had got a fright and scattered in all directions with their teachers frantically trying to get them together. This was my worst nightmare and as quickly as I could I checked if anyone was hurt but no one was. Bill got up looking decidedly green around the gills; he was in a mess but wasn't hurt. Between us we got everyone out of the game park and I left Bill closing the gate and hooking the padlock back into the lock. By now I knew I had a real problem: the two elephants were separated, something that always upset them. Rundi had disappeared from view and Muku, still inside the fence, blustered up and down, tail out, ears flapping, trumpeting hysterically in a high pitched squeal.

"I've got to get her back Bill," I called over my shoulder, leaving him calming down twenty children while I ran off to recover Rundi.

There wasn't a soul in sight to help me and I ran off in the direction I'd seen Rundi going, making a quick detour to a wild orange tree off the path, grabbing a ripe yellow fruit off the ground. Rounding a bend on the track I saw Rundi; she was a little way ahead of me, nearing the tea kiosk.

A dozen images flashed through my mind: the gate onto the main road was always open; would she go onto the road; would any of the workers see her; would there be traffic going past; how could I get in front of her? I knew that now I was in sight I mustn't run, I mustn't frighten her. Going a little closer until I guessed I was in her range of vision, I stood still and took a deep breath to calm myself.

"Rundi," I called out softly, my heart thumping.

She turned slightly and raised her trunk in my direction to catch my scent.

"Come Rundi." I stretched my arm out, offering her the wild orange. Rundi turned and took a small step towards me.

"That's it! Come on girl," I said, slowly bending and cracking open the fruit on the edge of a concrete picnic table. The familiar noise of the matamba breaking along with the intoxicating smell of the fruit got through to her and Rundi took a few more steps towards me. I scooped some of the thick brown pulp out of the matamba and held it out to her.

"Here Rundi," I whispered as she came closer and I lifted my hand with the fruit towards her. Rundi gently curled her trunk around my arm, guiding my hand into her mouth. She rumbled gently at me in a low, contented tone, staring straight into my eyes and I slowly moved a few steps back. I could see that her wild eyed fear of a moment before had subsided.

"Come on Rundi, let's go," I said quietly and breathed a huge sigh of relief as she followed me. Taking it calmly and gently we slowly made our way back down to the game park with me hand-feeding and talking to her quietly all the way. This was all completely new territory to Rundi, she had never seen this area of land before: manicured lawns and picnic tables, *Erythrina* and *Combretum* trees, ponds with fish and water lilies, tortoises, terrapins and crocodiles, huge Acacia trees and then, at last, the massive Fig tree that grew on the edge of the slope leading down to the game gate.

Luckily nothing distracted Rundi; she kept following me and I kept offering her slippery bits of matamba. Rundi was probably as shocked as I was and didn't hesitate to go back in through the gate, back to Muku and her territory. Muku immediately ran over to Rundi, rumbling and blowing air nosily out of his trunk and they rubbed heads before Muku gave Rundi a thorough smell inspection, sniffing her intently from the tips of her toes upwards.

Bill, his guests and the pre-school children were all up on the game viewing platform and when I looked up at them a little cheer and some clapping erupted. How very lucky I had been that Bill was there to help me and that no one got hurt. Rundi was back safe and sound, Muku was sucking on her ear and then Simon appeared with their buckets of milk and Raymond followed to help carry the vegetables in. Where on earth had they been all this time I wondered? It was incomprehensible that none of the workers had seen an escaped elephant or me chasing after her, not to mention twenty little children scattering in all directions.

I asked Ray to go back to the kiosk and bring me a box of ice cream cups for the children, a small way of making up for the big fright they had all got. As the elephants noisily sucked and slurped their milk and porridge, I wiped the sweat from my forehead and my hands were still shaking. While the children giggled, licked ice creams and mimicked elephants drinking with their noses from buckets, Bill brushed himself off. He looked a bit of a mess: red mud on white trousers and dirty splashes on his blue blazer but his two overseas guests were delighted at what had happened. This had been a real African Adventure for the foreigners and they hadn't lost their nerve but had switched on their video camera and caught the entire drama on film. Bill had remained totally in character and taken the whole thing in excellent humour; we were both quite shaken but very relieved that no one had got hurt. Some time later I heard that this story was re-told many times in the pub and Bill was known as the elephant man from the Jungle Book for many weeks afterwards!

A lot of lessons were learned that day, mostly by me, not the least of which was that Rundi and Muku were getting bigger and harder to control, something that game patroller Carolyn Dennison was also realising:

"The older Mukuvisi and Rundi got, the more they wanted to explore their surroundings. They were testing their strength all the time, pushing at trees, breaking off small branches and one of the things they seemed to take pleasure in doing, was breaking through the game fence into the public walking area of the Woodlands. They had minds of their own and often did not like being reprimanded for a misdemeanour, and would shake their heads, flap their ears and trumpet loudly!"

As funny and adorable as this all sounded, decision time was fast approaching and I planned to bring it up our next game committee meeting but a bit of Christmas cheer got in the way, as Margaret later recalled:

"We decided to have a party at the last meeting of the year. I brought two or three bottles of champagne, Sally had more South African red wine than we needed, Terry came with beer and we all brought snacks.

The champagne was hot, the wine was hot and it was a very hot day! I don't remember if we had a meeting, in fact I don't remember much of that day! We all got trashed: you, Sally, me, Beth, Terry and Carol. At one stage Beth had a paper snack plate on her head with bits of lettuce hanging off the edges. We all ended up lying under the big tree in star formation with dish cloths over our faces singing Christmas carols."

Beth and Peter Taylor had come to our Christmas meeting on Velosolex scooters and after our festivities, distinctly worse for wear they weaved away into the twilight after experiencing some difficulty in finding the gateway out of the car park.

THIRTEEN

....

Not long after the incident with Bill and the pre-schoolers, things suddenly started to change with the elephants. By early 1988 Rundi was two years old and Muku 26 months old. In elephant terms this is still early infancy because elephants live to sixty or more years, but Rundi and Muku were now almost as tall as me. They both had their tusks and for the first time I began to sometimes feel uncomfortable around them. Muku occasionally secreted fluid from his temporal glands and I soon learned that when you saw wet stains down the side of his face it was best to be more vigilant around him. I knew that this wasn't musth that indicates preparedness for sexual activity because Muku wasn't even a teenager yet; and it would be many years before he was ready to breed but something was definitely going on, the evidence ran down the sides of his face! Other members of the game committee also started recording seeing secretions from Muku's temporal glands and noticed that at the same time he would sometimes also drip urine while he was walking. We all soon learned that when Muku's glands were streaming his temperament was sometimes less predictable; the soft, gentle, placid Muku suddenly became a bit pushy. I began to become much more aware of the reality that the elephants had now almost outgrown the Mukuvisi Woodlands.

Rundi and Muku were getting bigger, not only in size but also in popularity. By 1988 internationally acclaimed author Gerald Durrell and artist David Shepherd were among their VIP visitors. Closer to home the Mukuvisi Woodlands was getting an increasing number of visitors including political and media personalities and always Rundi and Muku were the highlight, the star attraction. For Simon and me it was a never ending nightmare to be told that some famous person or other wanted to have their photograph taken with the elephants. So many things could go wrong, as I had found out far too often!

There were some requests that we didn't get into a flurry about at all because I just said no! The Sheraton Hotel which had opened in 1985 in Harare and specialized in hosting large public functions and conferences contacted me with one of the strangest requests I'd ever had. Arriving at work one morning I found a message on my desk to phone the public relations officer of the Sheraton Hotel.

"Hi," I said into the phone. "It's Cathy from the Mukuvisi Woodlands returning your call."

"Oh good!" answered this really smooth sounding man on the other end of the line.

The Sheraton Hotel was hosting the official launching of a new children's shampoo and the proceeds from the sale of the product were being donated to the nationwide Rhino Survival Campaign. It was always difficult to find something original to attract large numbers of people to such a function and that's when they thought of us.

"We were wondering if we could borrow your elephants for the night," the PR man said over the phone. "It would only be the one night and we will arrange all the transport and everything."

I was stunned and dumb struck. This had to be a joke.

"Hello? Cathy, are you still there?"

"Yes, I'm here but I'm really too busy for silly jokes right now," I replied brusquely and was about to hang up when the smooth voice stopped me:

"Oh no, this isn't a joke. I'm being serious; we would like to borrow your elephants for one night."

"Borrow our elephants for a night!" I echoed. "You can't be serious!"

"Just tell me how much you want; how about five hundred?"

"I'm sorry; I really don't know what you're talking about!"

"All right, a thousand then?"

"I'm sorry; it's totally out of the question!" I snapped, getting angrier by the minute.

"Now look Cathy, be reasonable, this is for charity you know. It's only the one night and all they will have to do is stand in the foyer."

"Stand in the foyer," I spluttered, "you want two elephants, to stand in the foyer of your hotel, under lights, with people milling all around and camera flashes popping in front of them. They're not toys you know, or domestic pets."

"Oh don't worry, we'll cordon them off with a couple of ropes and there will be plenty of food and water available."

This whole thing was ridiculous and I decided to put a stop to it right then.

"I'm really sorry Sir, the elephants are not for hire, for rent or for sale," I said and put the phone down.

Once I had calmed down a bit, I told Mike and Oscar the story and we all three rolled around with laughter at the thought of Rundi and Muku on display in the foyer of this fancy hotel. Great piles of dung splattering their walls, huge rivers of urine gushing across beautifully tiled floors and plush, fitted carpets; two flimsy little ropes holding back a tonne of irate flesh; it was too hysterical to even talk about.

Despite the absurdity of the request it made us all laugh, I couldn't believe how quickly and easily the man had suggested the money; was it a bribe and if not why did the offer double when I stood my ground? I felt sad for Rundi and Muku and the fate of all elephants like them that were rescued from culling. What was their place in Zimbabwe and what was their future? Would they really be able to live to sixty or more years like their wild relations? They were questions I couldn't answer but it didn't stop me thinking about them; thoughts that were soon interrupted when the next VIP was lined up, this time a personal one: my Mum! It was something of a shock to me to see how other people saw my relationship with two baby elephants. Mum wrote her memory of our afternoon walk early in the winter of 1988 in her journal:

"Catherine was the manager of a small wild life park in the middle of the city. So one of the first things to do was to see her domain and the two elephants she had hand-reared. I suppose you could say she had been their mother from the time they arrived at the park, two frightened little animals with the sounds and smells of the cull still fresh in their memories. And on one winter afternoon I met them for the first time. Catherine was perfectly at home with them but I felt distinctly nervous for they were very large. Rundi and Muku they were called, nearly two and a half years old but each weighing 450 kg. Not babies any more though still very loveable. One simply could not treat them like dogs to be called to 'heel.' Even though Catherine had reared them she knew enough to treat them with respect for the wild creatures that they really were. They were very used to humans and would tolerate the occasional slap on the rump from their 'mother' but it was unwise to take anything for granted with Rundi or Muku.

So it was with a fair amount of trepidation that I agreed when Catherine suggested the walk but I was very intrigued to see this daughter in her new role; I had seen her as a social worker, librarian, writer and teacher but this was very different. The plan was to walk the elephants to the other side of the game park, slip through the fence and then come home over the main road leaving the elephants to wander back on their own to the enclosure where they would find their evening meal. That was the plan. Perfect time, mid-afternoon, weather cool and pleasant.

ELEPHANT WALK
We can talk as we take the elephant walk
We can stroll along easy as they plod alongside

We can make our way home to fire and tea
Without hindrance or let from our heavyweight friends –
or that's what we thought!
But the rumbling beasts have other ideas,
and block every move with their wrinkled grey hides.
We try to advance they will not give way
but bump us and thump us and shove us aside.
So we'll follow we say, we'll follow in line:
Monarchs in front subjects behind!
But that does not please them;
Sulky and bulky in two-year-old tantrum they dawdle along...
To the left they see fruits juicy and lush,
We pause as they munch.
We watch and we wait and long now to leave
Day fades, sky darkens,
Chill wind rises and fear stirs.
Homeward traffic on the road
But no-one near to hear our calls.
Silently, stealthily seizing our chance,
We turn; they hear, they follow
...and the dance begins again.

Of course we got away in the end, though we had to take the long way and let them lead us back via their enclosure where they settled down for the night. It had been a strange experience, almost a tussle of love as if they knew who I was and resented me coming between them and their adopted mother. The strangeness was heightened by the fact that we were so near to the city with traffic and people all around while the little drama was being played out, as if we were enclosed in another reality."

Soon after the elephant walk with my Mum, news came that we were to have a visit from a national VIP, the Minister of Natural Resources and Tourism, Mrs Victoria Chitepo. This was a very high profile visitor for us and a very important one too and so our normal day to day tasks were put on hold while we prepared for the visit. It was a very busy time of year: winter was coming, fire break clearing was underway and Rundi and Muku were getting into more and more unplanned, unexpected situations by the day, challenging the fence, the gate and other animals. With eyes in the back of my head I got everyone together and we planned the spring cleaning ahead of the Minister's visit. Rain had been replaced by dust making cleaning an almost impossible task as the ceaseless wind whipped across the vlei in one direction and off the road in the other, carrying in blankets of dust all the time. One of the worst affected places was the Woodland Office situated on the edge of the car park. Each time a car drove in a cloud of dust would rise up and then drift down, settling gently on books, files and furniture in the office. We decided to dig a shallow ditch at the entrance to the car park so that vehicles would be forced to slow down and this would hopefully reduce the dust problem. Foolishly I gave the job of digging the ditch to Joçam.

"OK Joçam, do you understand?" I asked, after showing him where and how deep to dig the ditch across the road.

"Yes, yes, I see," Joçam said impatiently, grinning widely and nodding, the pick almost quivering in his hands.

Joçam, spat heartily on his hands, rubbed them together, hoisted the pick above his head and started breaking ground. I watched for a few minutes before leaving him to it, heading off into the game park to see how the fire breaks were getting on. I hadn't forgotten the dramas of the year before which had left Muku swinging a hoe over his head and casual workers hanging from the fence! The casual workers had made good progress with the job of clearing the strip around the fire break so far and it was now quite a walk to get to where they were. Rundi and Muku were nowhere in sight and when one of the men said they'd last been seen heading towards the back fence I decided to go and find them. The wire on the back fence was in a very bad state, rusty and weak, making it very easy for dogs to get in and elephants to get out. After finding Rundi and Muku and checking on the repaired bridge on the way back, it was some hours before I returned to the car park and office. I couldn't believe what Joçam had created in my absence.

Joçam came running in response to my call, his face creased in smiles.

"Joçam, what have you done?" I said pointing to the driveway.

Still grinning broadly Joçam said: "I see!" and as soon as he uttered those two words, I knew that he hadn't understood a word of what I had told him earlier.

"What do you mean 'you see' Joçam? Why have you dug such a deep ditch here Joçam? Cars are never going to be able to get through this crater!"

I knew that he didn't understand a single word I was saying. Taking a deep breath I started again: "This is too big Joçam, much too big. Look," I said and stepped into the trench. Joçam's speed dip was so deep that it came almost to my knees. "If I lie down here Joçam, this could even be a good grave, for me or you!"

"Very good," Joçam said, still with a wide grin stretched across his face.

This conversation was hopeless but I would have to do something about it fast. The first car that came in the gate would be swallowed up by the hole, probably have to be pulled out and would certainly wreck its suspension. Seeing Simon walking up I called out to him to bring a couple of shovels so that we could fix the damage.

With Simon and Joçam standing next to me I hefted the shovel and filled one part of the ditch until it was a mere dimple compared to Joçam's crater. With each shovel load, Joçam's grin melted and by the time I was done he looked truly crestfallen.

"Right," I said straightening up, wiping the sweat off my face; "this is how deep the dip should be. Do you see how I want it?"

Simon and Joçam nodded, I handed back the shovel and the dust flew as they hefted the soil back into the hole. I was annoyed with myself for having chosen Joçam for this job; he was always so over-zealous that I should have known that he would start a mine rather than dig a shallow dip. Joçam and Simon spent a long time re-filling the hole and trying to compact the ground again. We erected a sign warning of the dip and it took a while before some of our regular visitors got used to slowing down when they drove in. I would sit in the office and hold my breath as I heard cars bang and slam into the dip, suspension groaning, heads hitting the roofs of cabs. Fortunately the dip had flattened significantly by the time of Mrs Chitepo's visit, a great relief as a sore head would have been a very bad start to the afternoon.

The Minister arrived at the Woodlands with the inevitable entourage of journalists, photographers and TV camera crews and we spent some time showing her around and answering questions before making our way down to the game viewing platform. As we proceeded I glanced in the direction of the kiosk where Oscar and Ray were up to their eyes cutting delicate triangle sandwiches, slicing cakes and laying out the best crockery for later. Simon had been recruited to help at the kiosk until he was needed at the platform and he was busy filling up the urn before laying out chairs for the guests.

Mrs Chitepo had come to present a cheque to the Woodlands, which, for publicity reasons, had been enlarged and reinforced into a two metre long hardboard cheque, beautifully hand printed by the donors. As always I was glad that Peter Brookes-Ball was present to help me through the afternoon; he was far more practised at these public functions than I was and everything was going really well as we reached the platform and stood looking down at the two elephants. My heart went into my mouth when Minister Chitepo asked Peter if she could present the cheque inside the game park with the elephants standing in the background.

"That would be wonderful, wouldn't it Cathy?" Peter re-directed the question to me and suddenly a lot of people were looking at me, waiting for my answer. I felt distinctly uncomfortable and tried to explain that I couldn't guarantee that things would go according to plan.

"You never know what will happen with the elephants," I said, "they are wild animals."

How on earth was I going to get Rundi and Muku to stand politely in the background, behind the Minister while a cheque was being handed over? I had no answer to my own unspoken question. These elephants were never, ever in the background of any event. They loved being completely in the foreground of everything that was going on, in fact it was almost impossible to stop them. Mrs Chitepo chuckled as I tried to get out of this impending disaster and Peter smiled and gently patted me on the shoulder.

"Don't worry, it'll be fine," he whispered as I excused myself, muttering about needing to get keys.

I tried to leave gracefully, running the moment I was out of sight, stumbling to go and get Simon and Ray to come and help me. 'The Minister of Tourism meets the elephants!' what a wonderful headline and photograph that would be, not to mention excellent publicity for the Woodlands; but it could also be completely disastrous. As I ran, I sent up silent prayers that this would work and nothing would go wrong. I had been acutely embarrassed so many times in the past and although the incidents were funny in hindsight, they were a nightmare while they were happening. Arriving at the kiosk I gabbled out the plan to Simon and Ray and we walked back to the game viewing platform together. Ray went to get a good supply of horse cubes and Simon to fetch a sack of vegetables.

I knew it was best if we had plenty to keep the elephants busy when I took the Minister and reporters into the game area; if Rundi and Muku were busy at a pile of food there was a reasonable chance that nothing too dramatic would happen. As unethical as it was I'd also asked Simon to mix up another two buckets of milk and porridge to try and get the elephants as calm as possible. The elephants had their milk and porridge for the second time that day, accompanied by continuous camera clicking, laughter and exclamations of delight from the guests on the game viewing platform. Vegetables were spread out on the ground and horse cubes scattered around and then I led Mrs Chitepo into the game park.

All my fears about bad behaviour were groundless; perhaps Rundi and Muku sensed the importance of this very special guest or maybe they were just totally satisfied after the second round at the milk buckets that day. They behaved beautifully, held out almost clean trunks with just a small milky tidal ring and delicately but thoroughly inspected the Minister, sniffing her all over.

I don't really know how Simon managed to get Rundi and Muku to stand behind the Minister as she gave her televised speech but he did and I breathed another sigh of relief. There was one anxious moment when Rundi seemed intent on relieving Mrs Chitepo of the large cheque but Simon hastily put a stop to that. We had a wonderful afternoon with the Minister who impressed us all with her interest, concern and humour. She won Oscar's heart for life when she went un-announced into the back of the kiosk to wash her hands. Oscar was in a flurry to try and find her some scented soap which Mrs Chitepo brushed aside saying that she would use the familiar green laundry soap the same as anyone else!

Oscar soon forgot his delight with the Minister of Tourism using his green soap when he had an incident in the night.

"Please come quickly, there are burglars outside!"

That was the desperate, whispered plea from Oscar who phoned at 7pm on a Saturday evening. Oscar had been preparing his evening meal when he heard strange noises coming from the car park area. Not taking any chances, he snatched up his panga, crept down to the office and locked himself in to phone for help. Oscar sounded frantic on the phone, speaking so fast that he was almost incomprehensible. Suddenly he stopped gabbling, it went quiet for a couple of seconds.

"Wait, I see something, hold on."

"Oscar, be careful!" I urged but there was no one on the other end. I waited and when Oscar came back on the line, all the worry had gone out of his voice.

"It's the elephants," he chuckled, "Rundi and Muku are in the car park."

"OK Oscar, we're coming, don't try and chase them, just wait till we get there."

Ian and I went into immediate action; I grabbed half a dozen apples from the fruit basket, boots and a jersey; Ian got his torch and a jacket and we raced out of the house. I scrambled to pull on my boots and jersey while Ian drove, definitely breaking speed limits on the road to the Woodlands. As we drove up to the gates Ian switched off the lights and we left the car outside on the road. Oscar was waiting for us and while he re-locked the main gates behind us, I smashed the apples to pieces on the concrete step outside the office. We all grabbed handfuls of the soggy pulp before setting off to catch the escaped elephants. Once we were out of the beam of light from the office, it was dark, very dark and the moon wasn't up yet. Not daring to switch on the torch in case the light frightened the elephants, we made our way to the kiosk. Soft, slurping noises told us that we were heading in the right direction. As our eyes became accustomed to the dark and began to focus, I could feel a giggle bubbling up in my throat at the sight in front of us. There was Muku standing at the edge of the fish pond casually sucking up great trunk-fulls of water while Rundi was intent on stuffing as much of the lush lawn into her mouth as possible. I hoped Muku wasn't sucking up too many of our goldfish but stifled the fear induced giggles and took a deep breath.

"Rundi, Muku, come!" I called out softly.

I knew immediately that they had heard me. Rundi spread her ears and rumbled loudly while Muku swivelled his trunk in our direction and sniffed to ascertain our identity. Going towards the pair, we held out the sweet, mushy, irresistible pieces of apple. The fruit proved too much to resist and within seconds they were literally eating out of our hands. Half the battle was won. The problem now was to try and lure the elephants the four hundred or so metres down the path, past the crocodiles, behind the game viewing platform and back into the game park. The only way to do this was with food and the speed with which they were devouring the apples I could see we would need a lot of fruit to get them all the way down to the game gate; we needed to speed this up!

Leaving Ian and Oscar luring the elephants along the path with the apples, I raced ahead so as to get the gates into the game park open. The fruit was running out and within seconds I could hear the sound of apple-intoxicated elephants rapidly shuffling along on the path right behind me. I could almost feel their hot breath on the back of my neck and put on a burst of speed, running blindly down the path. I couldn't see much and hoped that I wouldn't trip on anything as the elephants would certainly trample me if I went down. At last I reached the gate and with infuriatingly shaking hands fumbled the key into the padlock, pulled the chain off and swung the gate open. Moments later, Oscar, Ian and the two elephants rushed past me and back into their huge playground where they were given the few remaining pieces of squashed apple. The three of us stood, panting and laughing, talking all at once in the adrenalin rush of a job well done. While Oscar went back up to the office to get some wire and turn the stove off under what must now be his burnt dinner, Ian and I found a sack of vegetables in the store-room and scattered the contents around for the elephants.

We still had to find and repair the hole in the fence, preferably without the help of the elephants. We switched on the torch and Rundi immediately went crazy: tail and ears out, she ran off crazily, trumpeting hysterically at the light. Luckily we didn't have to go far to find the damaged section of fence as it was only a few hundred metres away from the gate. The elephants had snapped three high-tension straining wires and pushed out ten metres of rusty mesh to secure their escape. By the light of a torch and Oscar's small, smoky paraffin lamp, we repaired the fence and by 9 pm the job was completed. What a way to spend Saturday evening! I knew that this was something we would have to get used to because Rundi and Muku had now learnt how easy it was to get out. The two not so baby elephants had suddenly discovered their own strength and in the process had learnt that being rescued was fun because it meant apples in the middle of the night!

The day after the elephant escape, I went to work very early to help Oscar clear away the evidence of the night time deed. In the hour or so that the elephants had been out, they uprooted and demolished a great deal of the lawn around the fish pond; the pond had to be topped up; the branches they had pulled down from small trees nearby were collected and put onto the compost heap and the balls of dung they had deposited everywhere had to be removed. As we cleared up Oscar and I talked.

"It's time isn't it Oscar?

"It is near," he replied.

Neither of us actually said the words that were on the tips of our tongues: it was time, nearly, for Rundi and Muku to leave the Woodlands.

The very day after the elephant escape, phone calls were made, money was released, orders were placed and within days work began on erecting the long overdue new game fence. Mine was one of many voices that had been agitating for a new game fence for a very long time.

We had held fund raising events, people had made donations, appeals had gone out to big businesses and at last the new fence was going to be erected. It would be some weeks before we could get all the way round the boundary with the new fence and in the meantime we had a problem. The elephants had got a taste for the grass on the other side of the fence, the irresistibly tempting greener pastures, and there was no stopping them now.

The next excursion was on a Friday night. This time it was Ray on the other end of the phone. Joggers on the main road had seen two elephants strolling along the railway line.

"Can you go straight away Ray, we'll be there shortly."

The railway line ran along the Transtobac Road boundary fence, heading west into the centre of the capital city, Harare, and east into the heart of the industrial areas. The gates onto the main road were locked and all the lights were off so Ian and I cruised slowly down the road, torch sweeping out the window, weaving from side to side, looking for elephants. If a policeman had stopped and asked us what we were doing I think we would have been arrested for drunk driving! As we went over the river bridge I heard a whistle and we pulled over and switched the engine off.

"Ray, is that you? Where are you?" I called out.

"Please help me!" a little voice called out of the darkness.

Ray had found both of the elephants and the hole in the fence. The problem was persuading them to go back through the hole. Muku had gone through the broken wire but Rundi was having none of it.

"What could I do?" Ray asked. "If I came to phone you to say where I was then maybe Rundi would have run away. I thought I better just stay here and wait. I knew you would come."

Ian and Ray stayed with Rundi at the hole in the fence while I ran along the road parallel to the fence until I got to the main gates, let myself in and went to get keys for the side gate and then ran back. I must have been gone for about twenty minutes and Rundi had obviously got bored of waiting. Turning the last corner I bumped into her and I don't know who got more of a fright.

"Rundi!" I exclaimed, holding my hand out to her.

Rundi's trunk came up and smelled me and then came her purring, rumbled greeting. Persuading her to turn round and follow me, we plodded along till we got to the side gate. Standing at my side Rundi waited patiently as I fiddled with the heavy lock and when the gate swung open she walked in quite happily with me and we were joined within a couple of minutes by Muku who was nonchalantly pulling out tufts of grass nearby. Leaving Ian and Ray to do yet another patch job on the fence I walked back to the platform with Rundi and Muku. Once again they were treated to night time rations of vegetables and cubes.

The next night we were again woken by the phone: the elephants were out again, this time in the car park. By the time we arrived Rundi and Muku had been out for quite a while, their balls of dung littering the car park. They had been up behind Oscar's house where they had demolished three banana trees, then down to their favourite spot, the fish pond. Here they had destroyed a clump of special ferns I had been nurturing and excavated quite a few holes in the lawn: scuffing up clods of the soft green grass with their feet before delicately shaking off the soil and eating them. We walked Rundi and Muku back to the game gate at the platform and rewarded them for their bad behaviour, again. I knew that if we didn't give them food once we got them back into the game park they would undoubtedly break back out almost immediately. When we finally found their escape hole, it was in exactly the same place as the night before; Rundi and Muku had simply followed the fence line all the way down to the car park and woken Oscar up to let them back in!

After that there was a phone call almost every night. Everyone's patience wore thin and tempers got shorter, enough was enough. We tried everything: sacks of vegetables tipped out at the platform at dusk, game cubes scattered in the grass near the pan, wheelbarrows full of banana leaves and reeds but nothing worked: Rundi and Muku had got a taste of the outside.

One Sunday afternoon Carolyn Dennison, who by then had been regaled with many of the tales of elephant escapes and apple rescues was on hand to help; an encounter that would be undoubtedly be told and retold to children and grandchildren for years to come!

"One Sunday afternoon people stopped in amazement as they encountered two elephants on Glenara Avenue. Some of them probably thought they had had too good a lunch! I got a frantic call to say Muku and Rundi had broken through the outside fence and were on the main road! I had an awful vision of them being run into by a big truck and with scarcely a thought, grabbed a packet of apples I had in the kitchen and rushed over the road (luckily I live very nearby).

There they were, the two miscreants, running up and down outside the fence, trumpeting loudly, throwing clouds of dust into the air and making mock-charging motions at some vehicles going past! I think they were actually a bit frightened being in an environment they knew nothing about and which looked quite scary, and were trying to show they were brave youngsters after all!

I ran towards them, calling their names as I approached the fence and waved the apples so they could get a good whiff. The combination of a human they knew and something that smelled nice seemed to work and the sight of me jogging along the fence-line waving apples closely followed by two elephants, must have given the crowd a good afternoon's entertainment! Luckily the staff had opened a gate and the elephants were soon back into the area by the game viewing platform which they knew well, and to my amusement and relief, within a minute they were happily chomping apples as if nothing had happened!"

It was a funny story indeed but what a tragedy it could have been if Carolyn hadn't been around that Sunday afternoon. The new game fence was still a long way from being finished, work was slow and the boundary was long. Oscar and I came up with a plan. We had been lucky so far that no one been hurt during the elephants' nocturnal outings and that they themselves hadn't been hurt. We knew that by not doing anything we were tempting fate; we had to stop the night time break outs before we had a disaster.

Oscar and I decided the only thing to do was to close the elephants in at night and the only suitable place was in their stable under the platform. It took five men to prepare the barricade: poles were cut and wired together to form a gate strong enough to secure the front of the stable. When it was all ready we laid out a gastronomic feast for the elephants and called them into their stable. We had collected a sack full of wild oranges, about sixty in all, armloads of guava branches, three full sacks of vegetables and of course a couple of buckets of cubes. Simon had prepared a giant, king size bed of straw piled a metre deep and there was a barrel of water outside the door but within trunk's reach. Rundi and Muku went in without any problem, not knowing what was going on and obviously unable to resist the feast that had been laid out for them. Neither of them reacted at all while the men slid poles across the doorway. Oscar wired the poles together and exhausted but satisfied we all went home, hoping to get a good night's sleep.

I didn't sleep much that night, tossing and turning and worrying about elephants locked in their bedroom. At 5.30 the next morning I pulled my clothes on and walked down to the Woodlands to let the elephants out. It was almost 6.00 am and awfully quiet when I got there and assuming that they were either sleeping or standing waiting at the door, I called out their names. There was no rumbled response; there couldn't be because Rundi and Muku had gone.

The two highest poles over the door had been pulled out and were lying in the straw. The next two poles, each as thick as a man's arm, were snapped in half as if they were matchsticks. The rest of the poles were in place so the elephants must have simply clambered over them to get out. Their stable was a mess; all the food was gone, the wooden shutter window had been smashed open and the drum of water outside the gate was lying on its side.

All manner of things went through my mind in an instant, uppermost was the thought that Rundi and Muku had hurt themselves during the break out; another was that they had got out onto the main road and were even now wandering around and heading into what would be early morning rush hour very soon. Then I saw them and a wave of relief flooded over me. Rundi and Muku were in the long grass by the boma. Muku was asleep, lying on his side in the grass and Rundi was asleep on her feet. I did not go to them then, but later in the day when I saw their wounds I realised the implications of what we had done by closing them in. Rundi had eighteen small cuts on her, mostly on her sides and a couple on her stomach. She had nasty cuts above both of her eyes and a deep wound on her neck with a hot swollen bruise on her head above her eyes. Muku had three small cuts on one of his sides but otherwise seemed fine. Rundi was quiet and lethargic and there was no doubt that she had done most, if not all of the work involved in breaking out of the stable. From the location and appearance of the cuts on Rundi, most of which were jagged tears, it seemed that she had done the damage to her head, eyes and face by smashing open the wooden, shutter window, injuring herself on sharp wooden splinters. It was hard to tell which of them had been involved in snapping the poles across the doorway. When I got the wound spray and tried to treat Rundi she went mad, screaming and bellowing before running away with Muku right behind her, both of them with their tails up and ears out. Suddenly I was the enemy.

After this I didn't try and close them in at night again and while work progressed on the fence Rundi and Muku continued to find weak spots in the wire and broke out almost every night. We made friends again and I reverted to putting huge piles of vegetables out for them last thing in the evening and then waiting for the inevitable phone call from Oscar or Ray. Large quantities of apples were always on my home grocery shopping list and a torch, jacket and track shoes were always at the ready near the back door: ready to go out on rescue missions. I knew the time had come; there was nothing for it, Rundi and Muku would have to go. In my heart I had always known this day would come and now I knew it would have to be soon.

FOURTEEN

....

Some time before Rundi and Muku began their nightly escapes I had made tentative plans for their relocation to a big game farm in Wedza and now I contacted Norman Travers to confirm the arrangement and make plans for their departure. Rundi and Muku had outgrown the Woodlands and I feared for their safety if they stayed at the Woodlands for much longer.

After many long telephone calls and letters, we finalized the relocation plans. In a way I was glad that Rundi and Muku were breaking out every night, it kept me so busy that there was no time to be emotional and sentimental about their impending departure. The Department of National Parks were happy about the relocation plans for Rundi and Muku and said they wanted us to rear two more baby elephants. By then elephants had become the life blood of the Woodlands, providing a unique learning opportunity for thousands of school children who attended our education programmes and also attracting countless tourists and visitors, keeping the Woodlands afloat every month. Despite the most incredible two years with Rundi and Muku I had very mixed feelings about the whole business and had more questions than answers. If culling had to happen shouldn't the entire herd be killed? Was it right to save individual elephant babies knowing that in the wild they always moved in large family groups where social interactions were central to every aspect of their lives? By taming these elephants weren't we making them easy targets for ivory poachers? Perhaps the greatest turmoil in my mind was the knowledge that elephants lived for sixty years: how could any of us say with confidence that by saving and hand rearing elephants they would have those sixty years?

The date for the arrival of two new baby elephants was set by National Parks and it was arranged that Rundi and Muku would leave the Woodlands a week before. As the day of the arrival of two new elephants drew nearer I was phoning Wedza almost every day to find out when they were coming to collect Rundi and Muku but the news wasn't good. Their truck had broken down and because you needed specialist transport to move elephants it looked like I was going to have two sets of elephants on my hands at the same time.

D Day arrived in the form of a phone call from Karoi to say that the truck with the two new baby elephants would be arriving at the Woodlands at 7pm that evening. I called an emergency meeting of all the workers. Top of the list of concerns was what to do with Rundi and Muku. They were enormous compared to the anticipated size of the new babies and there was no way the four elephants could be put together. If Rundi and Muku were staying at the Woodlands it would have been the most natural thing to put the calves together; an ideal solution was to have a small herd as this was exactly how they lived in the wild. But this wasn't the wild and nothing was natural or normal about hand rearing elephant calves whose herds had been culled; I had no option but to keep them apart for the few days that overlapped the arrivals and departures.

The biggest, strongest employee, Leonard, was immediately put on full time night duty. From then on his job was to keep Rundi and Muku away from the boma and to stay with them all night, not only to stop them breaking out, but to keep them from getting to the two new babies. Leonard was delighted with his new job, he pulled his massive shoulders back and went striding off to rest so that he could come back to work fresh and ready to start night shift that evening. All the other workers, led by Oscar headed off to the boma to get everything ready for the arrival of the two new elephant calves. Much of the preparatory work had already been done; the circular stockade had been checked, some poles replaced and the perimeter of the boma fence and its gate had been reinforced. A giant straw bed was laid out, water troughs were filled, leafy branches, a few vegetables, fruits and cubes were scattered around and everything was checked and double checked. We didn't know anything about the calves: how old they were, what sex they were or if they were even eating on their own yet. It wasn't until it was already dark that we heard the roar of a vehicle approaching; a big truck pulled into the car park and was directed to the loading ramp at the boma. Once the truck was in position which took some careful manoeuvring to ensure as small as possible a gap between truck and ramp, we were presented with the view of two large, grey backsides. It took half an hour of cursing, coaxing, persuading and cajoling before the two new baby elephants walked off the truck, down the ramp and along the boma corridor before they reached their new, safe home.

Not able to see or do anything once the elephants were in the ramp and knowing that Ian, Ray and Simon could manage, I went over to chat to the man who had accompanied the elephant truck from Karoi. Lauren Rambo had a big safari ranch in Karoi and he was the first to receive all the newly orphaned baby elephants after the National Parks culling operations. Because of the location of his property and the facilities he had established, Lauren was the first person the baby elephants came into contact with. These elephants being unloaded today had been rescued from culling operations in the Matusadona and surrounding areas and taken straight to Lauren's property where they were left to calm down for a few days before being sent out to their final destinations. I listened spellbound as Lauren told me the news about one of our own elephants. Coke, our big female elephant who had left the Woodlands when Rundi and Muku arrived, had gone to Lauren's ranch and she helped to settle the new babies when they arrived from the cull. Lauren said that Coke was now over two metres tall but she was still very tame and gentle and loved it when new baby elephants arrived. Coke would follow the new orphaned babies around, gently pushing them in the right direction when they tried to break out. Coke would rumble at them, sniff, nudge them and touch them all the time, just the way elephants in the wild did, constantly interacting with other members of the herd. Lauren said that Coke' presence undoubtedly had an enormously calming effect on these terrified, traumatised orphans. I was glad it was dark and that Lauren couldn't see the tears in my eyes as he talked.

Our two new elephants whom we later called Fungai (the thinker or listener) and Sango (from the wild) were as wild as ever. They charged at the boma ring paddock walls, bellowed, trumpeted, flapped their ears and raised clouds of dust at every turn. Simon was again in his element as he began working with the new elephants, another challenge for our famous elephant minder. Both elephants were covered in sores, scratches, bruises and cuts. They had deep suppurating rope burns on their legs where their feet had been tied together and the wounds oozed stinking pus, crawled with maggots and attracted hundreds of flies. Simon's dedication was unwavering and he worked day and night tending to his new babies, emerging at strange hours filthy, stinking and exhausted but always smiling because he was making progress. His work was beginning all over again with Fungai and Sango while mine was about to end with Rundi and Muku.

In their last days at the Mukuvisi Woodlands Rundi and Muku were almost never alone. Leonard continued his night patrols and I listened eagerly to his tales of what the elephants did at night, something we didn't have any knowledge of. Leonard said mostly the nights were uneventful, the elephants grazed or browsed, moving slowly and quietly, regularly checking (by touching) each other and Leonard with their trunks. They drank at the pan at 6pm and then not again until it was daylight the next morning. During the night they would feed for an hour or so and then sleep, usually standing up. These sleeps were brief periods of between fifteen and thirty minutes at a time. When they woke they would rumble, smell and touch each other and start feeding again. Leonard said that every night at around midnight Rundi and Muku would head back to the platform, check on what if any vegetables were lying around and then they would go into the stable under the platform, sleep for a little while, perhaps up to an hour, and then would emerge and wander back up the vlei and into the tree line.

On the 20th September 1988 Norman Travers phoned to say that his truck was repaired and elephant proof; he would be coming to fetch Rundi and Muku the next morning. The gnawing ache that had been at the bottom of my stomach for weeks began to churn.

The night before their departure from the Woodlands, Rundi and Muku gave Ian and I a wonderful performance. Leaving the platform just before dark, we turned back to take one last look and saw the elephants walking into the pan for a swim. They stood waist deep in the water, thrashing their trunks from side to side, pushing each other playfully and rumbling loudly. They were clearly relaxed and contented and abandoned themselves to their luxurious evening swim at the end of a hot, dry, dusty day. Rundi and Muku cavorted and rolled, flopped and splashed. They repeatedly nudged and nuzzled each other, trunks intertwined, tusks locked. A few times they submerged completely for a minute or more, churning up mud from the bottom leaving a dark brown stain in the water. The entire performance was accompanied by the sounds of pleasure: splashing, trumpeting and rumbling all of which drifted across the quiet evening and reached us at the platform.

The elephants stayed in the water for quarter of an hour and as the light faded they emerged and then slowly moved off into the night with Leonard following some way behind. Everything was coming to an end: my days with elephants and their days at the Woodlands.

On the 21st September 1988 Rundi and Muku left the Woodlands for their new home at Imire Game Park in Wedza. I recorded in my journal their departure from the Mukuvisi Woodlands:

"When the truck came at 10.30 in the morning we opened up the ramp and got the truck ready for her cargo. A beautiful bed of hay had been prepared for them closest to the cab and there were piles of cubes and lucerne scattered all over for them. They had their usual buckets of milk and porridge at the platform with Simon and he then he walked them unhurriedly to the boma. At last, after all these days, it was at this moment that Rundi and Muku apparently realized there were other elephants at the Woodlands. With Fungai and Sango securely out of reach in the boma's ring paddock, Rundi and Muku rumbled loudly to the other elephants. Fungai and Sango trumpeted and rumbled in response and their greeting was again returned by Rundi and Muku. This was so touching that a big lump rose in my throat. I swallowed hard, there was business to attend to and I wanted it over as soon as possible.

"By then a canvas roof had been secured over the roof bars of the truck and Rundi was called on first. She got on the truck and then went off, got on and off again and by the third attempt we were all getting very tense. The men were shouting at each other and the elephants were trumpeting a little. They were both manuring freely and as always in times of stress, it was a case of instant diarrhoea. Oscar suggested that I get in the truck and call them because they were not responding to anyone else. Not believing that it would work I asked everyone to keep very quiet and I got into the back of the truck, sat down in the hay and called to them, rumbling as I always did. Rundi stood in the doorway of the ramp, she put her trunk forward, smelled in my direction and then stepped into the truck, followed closely by Muku. As we had arranged earlier, Simon lifted in two buckets, each with an extra ration of milk and porridge and I indicated *that he should get in the truck with me. Rundi and Muku sucked up their milk as Simon and I stood holding their buckets for them and then I quietly retreated, telling Simon to stay with them so that they didn't get agitated again.*

"When I got off the truck Rundi and Muku were both quiet and still and Simon stayed talking his last loving words to them until the very end. As soon as we had finished tying down the tarpaulin the truck began to move slowly towards the road. Simon hung on till the last moment, only jumping off when the truck began accelerating. Tears ran down his face and I said something to try and comfort him but he just grumbled about going to his new babies and brushed past me."

For the rest of the day I agonised over how Rundi and Muku were, if they had arrived safely and wondering if the journey had been uneventful. As luck would have it the phone lines to Wedza were out of order and so there was nothing to do but wait and hope. Not able to think of anything else, I finally managed to get a line to Wedza at 7.30 that evening. The elephants had arrived safely, were fit and fine and had met Nyasha (the other elephant at Imire) and everyone was delighted. Rundi and Muku had got bored on the trip and finding a small hole in the canvas roof, had pulled and tugged until the truck's covering was well ventilated.

A week later Norman Travers came in to tell me about Rundi and Muku. They were fine and had settled in well. Norman said they were very tame and loving and very friendly towards Nyasha, following her everywhere. He said that Rundi and Muku were breaking out of their boma at Imire every night, exactly as they had done at the Woodlands but Norman wasn't worried.

I felt so proud and sad at the same time that Rundi and Muku had settled in so well and tolerated another enormous human interference in their young lives. I had given them the very best care that I could while they were in my charge and now they were the responsibility of someone else. I had no doubt that Norman Travers and his family would treat them with love and respect as they became adolescents and young elephants. Whether or not Rundi and Muku would stay together or even if they would stay at Imire for the rest of their lives (another sixty years) was not a question I could answer but I remembered the words of Morna Knottenbelt, the vet who treated them when they were babies at the Mukuvisi Woodlands. Morna had said that to survive in the wildlife industry there was one lesson you had to learn: the only thing that really mattered was how you treated the animal while it was in your care; what happened to the animal afterwards was out of your control.

Postscript

Ten years later, I went with Ian and our four-year-old son to Imire to see the elephants I had reared a decade before at the Mukuvisi Woodlands.

Imire were holding a big public function and hundreds of people had gathered for the event. I hadn't told Norman Travers I was coming and was apprehensive but also excited at the prospect of seeing Rundi and Muku again. Uppermost in my mind was whether they would recognise me or not. I felt so sure they would; after all don't they say an elephant never forgets?

Suddenly half a dozen elephants were there in front of us. Muku renamed Mac was out in the game park but there was no mistaking Rundi. There were crowds of people all around, dust, smoke from braai fires, noise and photographs but she behaved beautifully, not nervous or agitated, just standing calmly in her herd. I went a bit closer and there was no doubt: Rundi recognized me. She moved purposely towards me, rumbled loudly and put her trunk in my hair. I retreated, not wanting to upset her, but she followed, curled the bottom of her trunk and again laid it in my hair.

Goodbye Rundi, I whispered before turning and walking away.

Four elephants are being killed an hour. It's a race against time before we lose these gentle giants forever.
(Avaaz 2016)